NOMADS OF WESTERN TIBET

NOMADS OF WESTERN TIBET

THE SURVIVAL OF A WAY OF LIFE

Photography and text by
Melvyn C. Goldstein and Cynthia M. Beall

University of California Press
Berkeley   Los Angeles

Published in North and South America
by the University of California Press,
Berkeley, and Los Angeles, California

Library of Congress Cataloging-in-Publication Data

Goldstein, Melvyn C.
    Nomads of Western Tibet : the survival of a way of life /
photography and text by Melvyn C. Goldstein and Cynthia M. Beall.
        p.   cm.
    "First published by Odyssey Productions Ltd. . . . Hong Kong"—T.p.
verso.
    ISBN 0-520-07210-3. — ISBN 0-520-07211-1 (pbk.)
    1. Nomads—China—Tibet—Social life and customs. 2. Nomads
—China—Tibet—Economic conditions.   3. Nomads—Government policy
—China—Tibet. 4. Tibet (China)—Social life and customs.
I. Beall, Cynthia M.   II. Title
GN635.C5065   1990
305.9'0693—dc20   90-10882
                                                  CIP

DESIGNED BY David Hurst

Color separated and printed in Hong Kong
by Toppan Printing Co.
1 2 3 4 5 6 7 8 9

(Half -Title spread)   A Nomad drives his yak caravan home from a six-week trading trip laden with goods. Living at 16,000-17,500 feet on Tibet's awesome Northern Plateau, these nomadic pastoralists plant no crops. They subsist by rearing yak, sheep, goats, and horses, consuming some of their livestocks' products, and trading the rest for grain, tea, and other necessities.

(page 4)   This young woman wears a traditional winter hat made from the fleece of lambs that have died natural deaths. Her eye-catching jewelry is typical of this area and worn every day—not just on special occasions.

(pages 6 and 7)   A summer rainbow ends beside a herd of female yak heading home after a day of grazing. Nor is the generic term for yak and means "wealth." Yak actually refers only to castrated males, and dri is the nomads' name for female nor.

(opposite)   With the temperature still below zero, another winter day begins for a shepherd. Although bitterly cold, winter sees little precipitation and almost daily sunshine.

Women leave the warmth of their tents to start the morning's milking, a daily task regardless of the weather.

PREFACE

DECEMBER 11, 1987 WAS ANOTHER in an unbroken string of bitterly cold mornings on the *Changtang*, Tibet's vast "Northern Plateau." The wind whistled through the 16,500 foot-high nomad camp that was our home as the mid-morning sun struggled to raise the temperature—degree by degree—to 0°F. The temperature had reached minus 35°F the previous evening and, as was usual in winter, everything was frozen when we woke up—water, meat, toothbrushes. Our cook Sangbo continuously pumped a goat-skin hand bellows to aerate the dung fire glowing in the center of our small nomad-style tent. The sheep and goat pellets burned red hot, warming our front while our backs continued to feel the icy cold of winter through three layers of thermal underwear, a wool shirt, a bunting jacket and an expedition down coat. As the cook paused for a few minutes to churn a new pot of butter-tea, smoke from the waning fire began to fill the tent. We lumbered outside in our heavy gear to avoid the fumes and soak up the growing warmth of the sun in the crisp, fresh air.

In the distance a small caravan caught our eye—an old nomad, his two teenage sons and about 100 sheep laden with woolen saddle-bags filled with salt and butter. As their ancestors had done for untold centuries, these nomads were heading south to trade for grain with farmers living 20-30 days' distant. Wearing traditional sheep-fleece robes, fox-fur hats and two-foot-long swords stuck diagonally through their belts, the boys seemed absorbed in their thoughts, walking silently, occasionally using their slingshots to direct the course of the herd. Their father paid the boys no heed; he counted his rosary and chanted Buddhist prayers which the tumultuous wind carried across the plateau to the top of snowcapped Mt. Dargo where the local protective deities dwell. Farther east along the plain, a herd of several dozen wild asses noted their passing and then calmly resumed grazing on the dried grass. Not hunted by the nomads, they fear humans little in this part of the Changtang.

As the small caravan slowly vanished over the horizon, we marvelled not only that we were there conducting an in-depth anthropological study, but that the Changtang nomads' unique way of life was still intact and flourishing. The nomad caravan we watched on that cold and blustery morning could easily have been one described by Sven Hedin, the famous Swedish explorer who traversed Western Tibet in 1906–08 in an unsuccessful quest to reach Lhasa.

The Changtang, one of the least known, most remote and highest regions in the world, is home to 500,000 nomadic pastoralists.[2] Living for untold centuries at altitudes as high or higher than any other humans in the world, and inhabiting one of the world's harshest environments, Tibet's nomads have been able to wrest from their inhospitable environment a reliable source of food and products for both their own needs and for those of Tibet's elites. Their wool and yak tails were the primary sources of foreign exchange for the Kingdom of the Dalai Lamas, and still are a major component of the economy of the Tibet Autonomous Region [TAR].[3]

However, although nomadic pastoralism is still flourishing, the Changtang did not escape the changes wrought upon Tibet following the flight of the Dalai Lama in 1959 and Chinese assumption of direct administrative control. The nomads will not soon forget the ruthless, fanatic attempt to destroy their traditional culture and way of life during Mao Tse-tung's Great Proletarian Cultural Revolution, even though China's new (post-1980) policies have allowed revitalization of much of the traditional customs. The trials and tribulations experienced by the nomads, and their emergence intact from that nightmare, are as important to the story of the nomads of western Tibet as is the persistence of their ancient techniques of production and livestock management.

This book is a firsthand account of these remarkable people—their traditional way of life and their struggle for cultural survival. In a world where indigenous peoples and their environments are vanishing at alarming rates, the survival of this way of life represents an unexpected, but heartening, victory for all of humanity. Based on our 16 months of field research in Tibet between June 1986 and June 1988, 10 months of which we lived with one "community" of some 265 nomads, this book describes the traditional way of life of nomadic pastoralists in Western Tibet, their experiences under direct Chinese rule, and their current situation.

We decided early on that the best way to convey the life of these nomads would be to combine images with text, so made a concerted effort to record all aspects of their annual cycle on 35mm film. Generous help from the National Geographic Society allowed us to shoot almost 10,000 slides during all seasons. We have selected 212 photographs that represent not just a group of striking images, but a unique photographic documentary of the nomads' entire annual life cycle—their complete way of life.

Because the story of these nomads has interest far wider than our usual audience of scholars and students, we have written this account without anthropological jargon or the highly detailed discussions that typify a "technical" article or monograph. Despite this style, all that follows is based on our scientific research and the data we collected on the society, culture, history, biology and ecology of this rare branch of the human family tree.

Melvyn C. Goldstein and Cynthia M. Beall
Case Western Reserve University
Cleveland, Ohio
1 June 1989

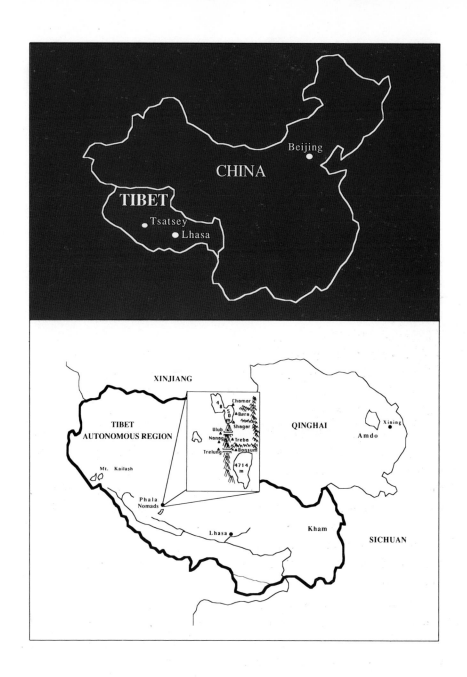

CONTENTS

OUR ARRIVAL IN NOMAD COUNTRY

After successfully concluding more than a year of negotiations, we left Lhasa, the capital of the Tibet Autonomous Region, in June 1986 to begin our study of the nomadic pastoralists of West Tibet. It was a dream come true.

Both of us already had considerable experience working with Tibetans outside of Tibet, but never expected to be the first anthropologists permitted to conduct in-depth ethnological fieldwork in Tibet itself. Goldstein, who first began studying Tibetan language and culture in 1960, recalls how the project came into being.

When China launched its new "open-door policy" in the early 1980s, I felt compelled to at least try to secure permission to conduct research in Tibet proper, and in 1982 proposed a study to assess recent linguistic and terminological change in Tibet to the Committee for Scholarly Communication with the People's Republic of China (the U.S. National Program for Advanced Research in China). As part of a bilateral cultural-exchange agreement between the U.S. and the People's Republic of China, it seemed the best hope for securing Chinese permission to do research in politically sensitive Tibet. The linguistic topic seemed appropriate since I had published a large Tibetan-English dictionary and two textbooks for studying Tibetan, and assumed that this would give credibility to my proposal in Beijing. The project was approved by the U.S. side in 1982, but was not acted on by the Chinese at this time. They did not reject the proposal, but instead enigmatically informed us that conditions in Tibet were not yet appropriate for inviting foreign researchers. It was not until the Spring of 1985, three years later, that I suddenly received a phone call from Washington saying, "The Chinese have finally approved your study and want you to come for two months—beginning as soon as possible." A few weeks later I was on my way to Lhasa.

More accustomed to carrying nomad tents than heavy metal boxes filled with scientific equipment, a yak caravan moves the authors' possessions from one nomad home-base to another.

During that first brief visit to Tibet, I was struck by the seeming vitality of nomad life in West Tibet. My hosts in Lhasa, at the Tibet Academy of Social Sciences (TASS), suggested I take a trip to see other parts of Tibet and I asked to visit West Tibet. In 1974 and 1976, I had conducted extended fieldwork with ethnic Tibetans in a remote part of northwest Nepal just across the border from West Tibet. During one of those research stints I had climbed up onto the mountain range that separated Nepal and Tibet and looked down into Tibet, frustrated that I could not descend with the local villagers and visit Tibet's holiest mountain, Mt. Kailash, which dominated the distant horizon. So when TASS offered me a trip, I immediately asked permission to visit Kailash, hoping I might also meet my old friends from Nepal who typically spend most of the summer trading in that part of Tibet. I left in a small jeep accompanied by my son Andre (a Chinese-language student at Beijing's People's University), several foul-smelling jerry cans full of gasoline which we would need when we crossed the wilderness areas, and a pleasant Tibetan driver named Kesang, who continuously puffed away on Chinese cigarettes, treating as silly our admonitions about the risk of igniting an explosion.

(above) At the end of a day, a household's dri (female yak) pause beside Two Sisters Lake.

(above right) Although several home-base camps are beside the lake, its water is too salty for human consumption, so they use water from small springs or glacier-fed streams.

(opposite) A mountain range separates Pala's 57 households into two sub-units. Here a yak caravan crosses a 17,500-foot pass and begins a descent to the Two Sisters' Lake at 16,000 feet.

The route to Mt. Kailash traversed nomad country for hundreds of miles, and we stopped daily at their tents to make tea and eat our midday meal. Although their dialect was difficult to understand, they seemed friendly and appeared to be still living the traditional life—many of the women, in fact, wore striking black makeup just as they had hundreds of years ago. The political climate in Tibet also seemed ripe for a major project, so when I returned to America I discussed the possibility of a joint field study of nomads with Cynthia Beall, a professor of physical anthropology at Case Western Reserve University who had conducted numerous studies of high-altitude populations both in the Andes and in Nepal. Beall, who spoke "rough and ready" Tibetan, was enthusiastic about the opportunity to extend her work in Nepal to Tibet where people live at higher elevations. We worked up a research plan and when I returned to Lhasa in the winter of 1985 to finish the language project, I presented our proposal (in Tibetan) to the Tibetan Academy of Social Sciences. The gods of Tibet must have been with us, for TASS seemed genuinely taken with the idea of a collaborative study of nomads. The hitch was that we wanted to live like nomads for a year in an area restricted to foreigners. TASS thought the Changtang was too difficult a place for us. "What would happen if you got seriously ill or fell off a horse and broke a bone?" they asked. "Why don't you just spend two summers there?"

(above) Sheep and goats comprise about 87% of the nomads' herds in this part of the Changtang.

(opposite, from top) The Changtang's weather changes rapidly and sudden storms may pelt the camp, herder, or weary traveler with hail, snow, sleet, or rain.

The Tibetan gazelle (gowa) are easily identified by the white tails. They are seen frequently around most nomad encampments.

Male yak transport heavy and bulky goods such as tents and wool. Impervious to snow and cold, they can traverse the highest passes.

Mel Goldstein signs the formal research agreement for the nomad project at the Tibet Academy of Social Sciences in Lhasa. Academy officials and scholars stand in the background.

I explained at length how the anthropological approach necessitates long-term immersion in a culture, and how we both had conducted fieldwork in Northwestern Nepal and regularly walked over rugged terrain for two weeks to reach the research sites, and how once there, we had eaten (and enjoyed) traditional Tibetan food. We later discovered that Kesang, the Kailash trip driver, had supported our claims to hardiness by telling people at TASS that my son and I were able to circumambulate Mt. Kailash on foot in one day just as Tibetan pilgrims do, leaving well before dawn and returning at 10:30 at night. Ultimately, TASS appreciated that our study design required living with the nomads during all seasons, and that we seemed tough enough to handle the altitudes and hardships, and they approved the project in principle.

When I returned to the U.S. in January of 1986, Cynthia and I worked feverishly to raise funding for the study, and with the help of the National Geographic Society's Committee for Exploration and Research, the National Academy of Science's Committee for Scholarly Communications with the People's Republic of China, and later the National Science Foundation and private companies which donated equipment, we were ready to begin our field research in 1986.

However, in May 1986, just as we were about to leave for Tibet, we received disappointing word from China that our program had to be formalized in a written agreement with Lhasa before they would issue us research visas. Knowing that it would be impossible to do this by mail, we decided to go to Lhasa anyway to negotiate the terms, hoping to start the research immediately afterwards.

The specific terms of the written agreement had to be worked out with the Tibet Academy of Social Sciences, our host institution which, in turn, had to secure permission from the government of the TAR. We wasted no time on sightseeing, and two days after we arrived in Lhasa, began a series of meetings to finalize an agreement. Negotiations ultimately took a whole month: this was TASS's first formal research agreement with Western scholars and there were many issues to hammer

out. Initially, for example, they suggested that we turn over all our field notes to them and then ask for sections back as we needed them to write up the study. We, of course, politely refused, saying that we had to have complete access to all of our data. Ultimately, all issues were resolved to our mutual satisfaction and the agreement was signed at a formal ceremony complete with toasts and a photographer in an elegant room with Tibetan carpets and furnishings.

21

(above) Tibetan nomads convert perishable milk into butter by transforming it into yogurt. The first step in this process is to bring the milk to a boil as is being done here. The iron tripod on which the milk sits was obtained from villagers who barter such products for live sheep and goats, wool and skins.

(opposite) Smoke from the fire swirls toward the open tent roof as this woman pours boiled tea from a metal pot into a wooden tea churn already holding salt and butter for Tibetan tea.

TIBETAN TEA

Tea made with salt and butter is one of Tibet's most unusual foods. Nomads and villagers drink tea throughout the day, and contrary to what one might imagine, it is very tasty.

The unusual tea comes from inland China, compressed into rock-hard balls or bricks which keep for decades. It is not uncommon to need a knife to break or chip off a part for use.

A handful is crumbled into a pot of water and boiled until it takes on a deep brown color. Tea leaves are reboiled several times, and eventually become horse fodder. Although the nomads do drink this tea plain with just salt, typically they pour it into a small wooden churn together with a handful of salt and a lump of butter and aerate the mixture with a wooden plunger. The tan-colored "tea-salt-butter" mixture is poured into a clay or metal teapot for serving. The oft-repeated comment that Tibetans particularly appreciate rancid butter in their tea is one of the ridiculously untrue myths about Tibet. Fresh butter is used when it is available. They may also use oil if no butter is available.

We drank this tea regularly and enjoyed it, although it tastes more like a Western-style broth than anything we would recognize as "tea" in a blindfold test. We particularly appreciated it in cold weather, for it seemed to warm to the core in a way our own tea did not.

One day soon after we arrived, a couple of nomad women from our encampment stopped by our tent just as Cynthia was making some Darjeeling tea. Fascinated by the shiny stainless-steel tea ball, they asked her what she was doing. She explained and offered them a taste. After the first sip they thought a bit, whispered something to each other, and then asked our cook for some salt which they added to their cups. After their second sip, smiles emerged and they nodded, informing us that our tea was really not bad at all—it just needed a dash of salt.

Having been packed for weeks, we departed for the field the day after the formal signing ceremony. Sonam, an official from TASS, and Lobsang, our research assistant, accompanied us to Tsatsey (pronounced tsa-tsay) district, the area 300 miles northwest of Lhasa we had selected to study.

Sonam was from an aristocratic family that had been sympathetic to the Chinese and their reforms from early on. As a youth, he had been a soldier in Tibet in the People's Liberation Army, and had served as an official in a nomad area adjacent to Tsatsey during the Cultural Revolution (in the 1970s). His experience in nomad country provided us helpful information on the events that had transpired there following the Chinese assumption of control over Tibet in 1959, and invaluable insights into what life would be like.

Lobsang, on the other hand, was not a government official or "cadre," as they call them in China. He was one of "the masses" (*mangtso*), i.e., from the common people. Although he spoke not a word of English and his education had stopped at middle school, he was a true intellectual with an alert and inquisitive mind. In his forties, he had retired early from his job as the accountant of a Lhasa cooperative business and was engaged in small business when we met him through a mutual Lhasa friend. He fulfilled all our requirements for a research assistant: he was intelligent, outgoing, verbal, and able to interact comfortably with all levels and classes of society. Moreover, in the early 1960s he had lived in Northern Tibet in a labor camp mining borax, so we did not have to worry about his ability to withstand the rigors of life in tents in nomad country.

Two days of travel from Lhasa in a Toyota Landcruiser took us southwest to Shigatse, Tibet's second largest city, and then due west to Ngamring, the county seat of the nomad area we had chosen. The current administrative structure of the Tibet Autonomous Region [TAR] consists of seven large administrative units called "prefectures," each containing some of Tibet's 77 "counties" (*shen*). These, in turn, are made up of "districts" (called *chü*) containing "villages" (*shang*). Ngamring, located in Shigatse prefecture, is a relatively large county seat that includes a high school and several score of government offices.

Ngamring's leading officials met with us in the county's large conference room. Bright red Tibetan-style coffee tables were lined up in front of the several black plastic upholstered couches along each of three sides of the room; a pot-belly stove sat in the center of the room. On one wall, three large framed pictures of Marx, Lenin, and Mao hung fading, a strange juxtaposition with the colorful tables and bright new Tibetan carpets draped over each couch. We all sat down and were served Chinese-style loose green tea in spotless porcelain cups, each with a matching lid.

The officials, all Tibetan but one, knew we were coming to conduct research with nomadic pastoralists, and asked which of the three nomadic pastoral districts under Ngamring we were planning to visit and how long we planned to stay. We explained our intentions and also answered a number of questions about America—for example, whether it was really true that everyone had his own automobile. In turn, we asked them many questions about the climate, roads, and differences among their three nomad districts. They had never dreamed that foreigners would have studied their language and be able to communicate with them in Tibetan, and seemed not only impressed, but proud. Our presentation went well and early the next morning, our third day out from Lhasa, we left for Tsatsey, one of three district headquarters in Ngamring and one of the hundreds of isolated district headquarters in the vast nomad country that covers the western and northwestern Changtang of the TAR. After traveling about 60 miles westward on Tibet's main east-west road, we reached Sangsang, a sleepy district headquarters where we stopped for a cup of Tibetan tea at the house of the school principal (a former nomad himself) who was a good friend of Sonam, the Tibet Academy of Social Sciences' representative.

Sangsang is located at 14,600 feet in the center of a large pastoral district bisected by Tibet's main east-west motor road. This road is key to Tibet's communications infrastructure, linking the Ali (Ngari) Prefecture, which sits in the west on the hostile Indian border, with the rest of Tibet. It is unpaved, although some sections of it are maintained by donkey-drawn carts that pull scrapers to level the surface and by road crews that shovel dirt and stones on or off the road as appropriate. However, it is really nothing more than a rough rural dirt road in the U.S.

After an hour of conversation, dry meat, and hot tea, we left Sangsang and the main road, traveling north on a rugged, unimproved, and unmarked dirt track. We passed nothing but ranges of snowcapped peaks, herds of gazelle and wild asses, and one or two nomad tents. Our research design required a relatively remote area away from the heavily traveled road so that we could study nomadic pastoralism in a community that had not been altered by special development projects or by the road itself. As we had hoped, this area seemed perfect, for it was clearly not some "showcase" nomad area.

We intended to conduct our study in one of Tsatsey's eight nomad groups (shang), but needed more information about the eight in order to decide which would serve our needs best. So we planned to stay overnight in Tsatsey's district headquarters to discuss this with the officials there. We were on a tight schedule because the representative from TASS had to return to Lhasa that next day with the car to help host a close relative of the King of Nepal.

As luck would have it, the drive from Sangsang took longer than expected because we missed a turn and drove in the wrong direction for a couple of hours. There is no road *per se* in this area and one simply drives on the plains trying to follow the faint tracks of the last car or truck that passed by. The vague instructions we received at Sangsang said only to turn west after several hours driving and go just south of a rounded snowcapped peak, crossing a river and a small bridge. After three hours of travel north, we suspected we were lost, but we encountered no one whom we could ask for another two hours. Finally we spied a lone tent and stopped to ask where we were. The old nomad woman living there laughed when she heard that we were headed for Tsatsey. Informing us that we were actually in Tshome district, she pointed south and said that the road to Tsatsey veered west a long ways back.

She made us some tea and we dug into our *tsamba* bag and made a quick meal.

(above) Butter-tea is occasionally prepared right in the teapot by twirling a small wooden paddle between the palms. The woman's 76-year-old mother came to live with her a few years earlier after she became blind. She spends most of her time counting prayers on her rosary or turning the prayer wheel which is hanging on the wall of the tent.

(left) The plains of the Western Changtang are crisscrossed by mountain ranges and ridges. A traveler unfamiliar with the locale could easily miss the small nomad home-base camp in the background.

After the meal, we backtracked, found the junction and finally arrived at the Tsatsey headquarters shortly after sunset, at 10:30 p.m. Located in the middle of a large flat plain where the nomads' headman used to live in the pre-Chinese days, Tsatsey consists of four large compounds, one for officials, one for the store and trade offices, one for a clinic, and one for the primary school. Each compound contains a square of one-story attached rooms surrounding a spacious courtyard large enough to hold six to eight trucks or a long yak caravan.

Our Landcruiser pulled into a dark, deserted courtyard that reminded us of a U.S. ghost town. The wind was awful, the swirling dust forcing us to shield our eyes as we set about finding the Tsatsey officials. It turned out that they were all at a party and, if truth be told, seemed to have had quite a bit to drink. When they first saw us in the poor light of a fading gasoline lamp, they responded with a shocked reserve bordering on hostility. However, once they realized that the Lhasa official from TASS was none other than Sonam, their old friend from Sangsang, and that we had permission to be there, their attitude changed completely and we were treated like visiting dignitaries.

Dorje, the district head, escorted us to the visitors' quarters. Wedged into a low mud-brick room with a single tiny window were five knee-high wooden bed frames each with two rolled-up quilts and a pillow adorned with a small towel as is current Chinese custom. A pot-bellied iron dung-burning stove with a crooked chimney sat in the middle, almost touching two of the beds. Dorje lent us a lamp, gave us a thermos of hot Tibetan tea together with a leg of antelope meat to boil for dinner, and saw to it that a sackful of dry yak-dung patties was delivered.

While the antelope meat simmered in the wee hours of that night, he took us to the quarters of his colleague, the communist party chairman, to discuss each of Tsatsey's eight nomad units so that we could select the one most appropriate for our research. Both officials were Tibetans, and the conversation was entirely in Tibetan. We later ascertained that there were no Han (ethnic Chinese) officials in Tsatsey and that Tibetan was the mode of communication even for official correspondence and records. We stayed up late that night asking questions and narrowing down the choices because the car had to leave the next evening and we wanted to transport our equipment and food to one of Tsatsey's eight nomad groups before it left. But choosing an area was difficult—some had more households, or more goats, or more sheep, but all seemed very similar. Ultimately, we selected what we thought was an "average" community—one that was neither the richest nor the poorest in the area, as well as two back-up sites in case the first proved unsatisfactory for some unforeseen reason. No restrictions were placed on which group or groups within Tsatsey we lived and worked with.

TSAMBA

Tsamba, the nomads' staple food, is ground barley that looks and feels like flour, although it has been popped (like popcorn) and is thus edible without further processing. It provides about half of the nomads' calories.

Preparation begins with wetting the raw barley kernels and tossing them, a few handfuls at a time, onto sand which has been heated to a high temperature. A few seconds of tossing the kernels with the heated sand pops them without scorching since the sand diffuses the heat evenly. Pouring the mixture into a sieve separates the popped barley (called *yö*) from the sand. For grinding, the popped kernels are fed through a hole in the center of the upper of two flat round stones making up the hand mill. Each of these stones weighs about 30-50 pounds and is about 15 inches in diameter. The resultant white "flour," called *tsamba*, spills out from between the stones onto a large cloth or hide placed under the mill. Milling is done every other day or so because the nomads prepare only a small supply (a few pounds) at a time, preferring to eat "fresh-ground" *tsamba*.

As a light snack, *tsamba* is eaten dry by pouring a spoonful on the tongue where it gradually becomes wet from saliva. Until we became used to this style of eating, we often embarrassed ourselves with fits of coughing after accidentally inhaling some of the dry *tsamba*. We quickly learned not to talk or even breathe (inhale) until the dry *tsamba* got wet. To make a more filling meal, Tibetans mix a little tea into their *tsamba* and knead it with their right hand, all the while turning the bowl with their left. The result is a stiff dough-like ball that is called *ba*. *Tsamba* is also mixed with enough tea to make a concoction the consistency of cooked oatmeal.

The barley flavor is often enhanced by the addition of butter, dried cheese, and even a dried molasses imported from Nepal known as *gurum*. Or a layer of yogurt might be added on top of the *tsamba* and then licked off and another added, until the *tsamba* is finished.

We usually ate one or another form of *tsamba* for breakfast and lunch, and then ate rice or unleavened bread for dinner. So as not to strain the nomads' resources, we brought all our food from Lhasa, except for yogurt and meat which we bought when it was plentiful. *Tsamba* is a great trail food because it requires no further cooking and can be eaten with plain water if it is not feasible to make a fire and tea, for example during a storm. Eaten with dried cheese and meat, it provides a highly nutritious meal that requires virtually no preparation and at most, one pot to boil water.

The nomads heat sand to pop the barley because it disperses the heat evenly and prevents the kernels from burning. Both mud-clay hearths and iron tripods are used as stoves. Sieves separate the barley from the sand. The popped barley is ground on a hand mill made of stone.

(opposite) Village and urban Tibetans consider the Changtang an extremely dangerous place, but the nomads know its every ridge and plain and think nothing of going on two- to three-week trips alone.

Tibetan gazelles (gowa) graze in early-morning sunlight only a few hundred yards from a nomadic campsite.

Economically, sheep are the nomads' most valuable animal. They provide meat, wool, and the skins and fleece that are used for their 20-pound winter robes.

(pages 32–33) The nomads' traditional pastoral subsistence system has enabled them to live on the Changtang for centuries despite the bleak environment and a brief four-month growing season.

Early the next morning we squeezed back into the Landcruiser, accompanied by Dorje, who had graciously agreed to introduce us personally to the community. It was normally a four- to five-hour trip, but again we encountered problems. While driving across what looked like a frozen river, one of our wheels broke through the ice, leaving us stuck in the middle of the river, halfway up a mountain pass at 17,100 feet. We were devastated since we knew that unless we freed the car quickly, there would not be enough time for it to take us farther and we would either have to go back to Tsatsey and start off again with a yak caravan, or wait where we were while Dorje returned and sent us yaks from Tsatsey. Having already wasted a month of research time in Lhasa negotiating the agreement, we had visions of wasting another two weeks: although we were only two or three hours away from our destination by car, it would take three to four days of travel by yak caravan once we managed to round up enough animals, a task that would certainly take at least another seven to 10 days.

With the rays of the blazing sun reflecting off the ice and snow, we spent several hours pushing, pulling, and rocking the car in a futile attempt to free it, gradually unloading our gear—tents, tent poles, sleeping bags, and food—to lighten the car. Finally, Dorje walked an hour to a nomad camp we had seen on the way up, while we scouted around to see if there was enough fuel (dung) lying around to allow us to camp there if necessary. Dorje returned with some nomads who helped us extricate ourselves after another hour or two of jacking up the car, pulling it a foot, and then repeating the process. It was hard and slow work, and by the time we freed ourselves, our fears were realized—it was too late to reach the site that was our first choice (see photo, p. 190).

(below left) Women keep the fire going with skin bellows as a young man has his hair braided. The household's possessions are piled along the tent wall and covered with homespun and woven wool blankets.

(below) In summer, women milk goats (and sheep) twice a day and milk is abundant. This time of plenty lasts just from June to September when both sheep and goats go dry.

34

Our driver wanted to return to Tsatsey immediately and leave us to move by yak from there. We tried to persuade him to take us farther. At this junction, Dorje remarked that once we crossed the pass, one of our second choices, the area known as Pala, was less than an hour away. The driver then reluctantly agreed to drop us there and, as the sun descended toward the horizon, we crossed the Parong Pass (17,500 feet) and descended into a valley several miles wide that was ringed with snowcapped peaks. Again there was no road per se, so we drove across the valley floor moving toward a spectacular sapphire-blue lake that we later learned was called Motso Pünnyi, "Two Sisters" lake. Our destination that evening was a small encampment of three black yak-hair tents pitched about a quarter mile in front of the lake. We planned to stay there for a few days while we organized a yak caravan to move us to our intended site three days distant.

At the unusual sound of the approaching vehicle, people rushed out of their tents and were astonished at the sight of two foreigners accompanying Dorje. Invited in, we sat down, as custom dictated, to the right of the fire blazing in the center of the tent. Trinley, a 63-year-old nomad, was minding the fire, aromatic smoke whirling around his head as he pumped his goatskin bellow to keep it burning hot. Because there are no trees or shrubs on the Changtang, yak, sheep and goat dung are used for fuel. As we would gradually come to understand, these nomads most often use goat and sheep dung (called *rima* in Tibetan) because it is more plentiful than yak dung and burns hotter. However, unlike yak dung which will burn by itself once it is ignited, *rima* requires aeration from a bellows to keep it burning.

We learned that we were the first Westerners they had ever seen, and were not surprised when Trinley stared at us curiously while another nomad moved about offering us traditional nomad hospitality—Tibetan tea, yogurt, and *tsamba*.

(above left) The nomads use yak, sheep, and goat dung for fuel because there are no trees on the Changtang. Dry yak dung is gathered in a wool bag to carry back to camp.

A fresh layer is added to a growing mound of dried yak dung that will be left at this site until the family returns in a few months.

(above) winnowing dry sheep/goat dung
by slowly sifting it through the hands

(right) The dried dung is poured slowly
from a pan so that the wind separates the
dirt and dust.

(left) coaxing a goat to drink some home-brew medicine

(below) sheep not only provide meat, milk, wool and skins, but also carry loads of up to 30 pounds.

Serving tea to guests is a universal form of Tibetan hospitality, and travelers always carry small wooden drinking bowls called *poba* in their pockets since hosts are not expected to provide cups for visitors. When the host offers tea, the guest places his or her bowl on a small foot-high table (or stone or piece of sod). Nomad etiquette calls for leaving the newly filled cup untouched until the host returns with the teapot to offer more. By this time the tea has cooled somewhat and the butter has separated forming a thin layer on top of the tea. The guest then blows away a patch of butter to reveal the dark liquid beneath, takes a large gulp of the tea, and sets the cup down again so that the waiting host can refill it. Then it sits again until the next offer to replenish it. Both of us had drunk Tibetan tea before and liked it, but were surprised by our first experience with Pala nomad tea because the flavor was very strong, almost bitter, and there was very little salt compared to Lhasa tea. We later learned that nomad tea contains only about half the salt and butter of standard Lhasa tea. So different were the nomad and Lhasa teas that in the ensuing months when we occasionally hired nomads to pump the bellows for our fires, they brought tea from their own tent rather than drink the tea made by our Lhasa assistant, which they found too salty.

After a few cups of tea and some small talk and jokes about "Imperialist America," the "paper tiger" they had heard criticized frequently during the Cultural Revolution, we explained that we planned to study the nomadic pastoral way of life by living with Tsatsey nomads during all seasons in the coming year and a half. As they heard our plan, a look of incredulity appeared on Trinley's face. He stopped pumping his bellows and said hesitantly, "But it is not possible for you to live here on the Changtang in tents. It is bitterly cold and windy in winter, and only we, the *drokba* (nomads),[4] can survive here."

Elaborating in excruciatingly vivid detail about the bitter cold, he again said proudly that only the *drokba* can cope. We, in turn, assured him (without much conviction) that it is very cold and snowy at our "encampment" in Cleveland, where we both teach in the Department of Anthropology at Case Western Reserve University. He seemed amused to hear that it snowed in America, but was clearly unconvinced.

(above) Standing out against the white background of a snowstorm, this breeding yak (called bo-a) is easily identified by his size and long, uncut belly hair (called dziba).

(opposite above) A 10-year-old herder bundled up to leave with the animals on a freezing winter morning. His cloak is made from 8 to 10 sheepskins and is worn with the fleece on the inside. The long sleeves function as mittens. Herders get no hot food while they are out and say that on the coldest days their faces become so numb that when they return in the evening they cannot talk until they warm up in the tent.

(opposite) The nomads' tents are made from woven yak hair cloth and afford them excellent protection from wind and snow. However, once the fire goes out at night, the temperature inside the tent falls to that outside.

(left) Once the nomads break camp, neither snow nor hail nor frigid streams deter them.

After that somewhat pessimistic evaluation of our prospects, Dorje and the other TASS official left in the Toyota Landcruiser, and we set up our first night's camp by moonlight, beginning our study of the inhabitants of one of the world's last scientific frontiers—the awesome Changtang.

In the next few days, as we began to discuss our plans with Trinley and the other nomads in the encampment, we not only found them wonderfully open and friendly, but also discovered that the group that was our first choice for a research site would be less appropriate than we thought since it was actually the second richest area in Tsatsey. Consequently, after camping five days beside stunning Two Sisters Lake, talking to the nomads and pondering the options, we concluded that although Pala's 10 home-base encampments (263 persons and 57 households) were a little smaller than we originally desired, it was otherwise perfect, and decided to make it our research site. It was a decision we have never regretted.

Throughout the duration of our study the Pala nomads were extremely cooperative and, as it turned out, our initial plan to study an area larger than Pala was overly optimistic. The nomads' encampments are scattered over several hundred square miles and visiting them repeatedly was a challenge. We had to cross three mountain passes 17,500 feet or higher to reach all 10 of Pala's major encampments, and one circuit of all the encampments could easily take 40 days since much time was wasted rounding up the carrying yaks.

THE CHANGTANG AND NOMADIC PASTORALISM

DESPITE ITS NAME OF "NORTHERN PLATEAU," the western section of the Changtang is not a vast level plain but a myriad of valleys and plains of varying sizes separated by twisting mountain ridges which transect the land. Located in central and north Tibet, the Changtang contains about 69% of Tibet's land mass, spanning a thousand miles from the Indian state of Ladakh in the west to the Chinese province of Qinghai in the east. This majestic plateau is home to millions of head of domestic livestock, and about 25% of the TAR's total population of nearly two million people.

Nomadic pastoralism as a way of life developed relatively late in human history, arising only about 9,000-10,000 years ago in Southwest Asia at roughly the same time as agriculture. The earliest nomadic pastoralists lived in Southwest Asia, herding mostly sheep and goats. Slightly later, there is evidence in South Asia of a sizable cattle-herding culture. Tibet's nomads represent one of the last great examples of the nomadic pastoral way of life once common in many regions of the world.

It is not known when nomadic pastoralism first emerged in Tibet, but it is doubtful that large-scale nomadic pastoralism was possible prior to the domestication of the wild yak (known as *Bos mutus* or *drong* in Tibetan). This magnificent beast, related to the ox and our own domestic cow, is enormous. Males are typically six feet high at the shoulders, and their horns are so large that they are hollowed and used as containers to hold home-brewed barley beer. Unfortunately, archaeological research in Tibet is in its infancy and little is known about the domestication of the yak or the origins of nomadic pastoralism there, but it is not unlikely that domestication of the wild yak took place on the Tibetan Changtang where it is still found in its greatest numbers.

Lightweight cloth traveling (or "satellite") tents are pitched at a transient campsite in summer vegetation.

Dwarfed by the Changtang's bleak mountains, the nomads pursue their traditional way of life. Under China's new economic and cultural policies, the hated commune was ended in 1981 and all its livestock divided among the nomads, the household again becoming the basic unit of production and consumption.

(right) For 8 to 9 months of the year the livestock graze on dried vegetation left standing at the end of the growing season. The golden hues of the dried grass look beautiful, but this is actually the most dangerous time for the nomads. A sudden heavy snowstorm can cloak the grasses and sedges with a thick layer of snow that freezes and prevents the livestock from feeding. With no stores of fodder to substitute, a family's herd can be decimated in a matter of days. Fortunately, heavy storms are rare and the intense sun usually reappears the next day and melts the snow.

The nomads of Pala are the descendents of these early yak-herding nomads who, perhaps several thousand years ago, began to move their herds around the Changtang where they captured the energy locked in the wild grasses and converted it into food, clothing and shelter.

Nomadic pastoralism continues to flourish in Tibet because the nomads have no competitors, unlike the other well-known traditional nomadic areas in Southwest Asia (Iran, Turkey, Afghanistan, Pakistan) and Africa. There, farmers have encroached on nomadic pasturelands and, with the help of governments hostile to the nomadic way of life, driven the nomadic pastoralists into progressively more marginal lands, often forcing them to emigrate and take work in the non-pastoral economy. Here, however, the extreme high altitude and bitter climate of the Tibetan Changtang have effectively precluded agriculture as an economic alternative, even with today's technology. Not only is the growing season too short for crops, but the weather is far too unpredictable. For example, every afternoon for two weeks in mid-August 1987, we experienced violent hail storms which would certainly have destroyed a ripening grain crop. If there were no nomads to utilize the high plateau in Tibet, it would revert to the wild fauna, not to other humans. Successive governments in Tibet have sought to control the Changtang's nomads and their products, not displace them.

(above) Two long interdigitating lines of goats tied for milking. The orange dye indicates ownership. The nomads have a clear-cut division of labor. Women are mainly responsible for milking, butter making, and camp work, while the men do the traveling and trading.

(left) Precipitation in Pala is monsoonal. From late June to September moisture-laden winds blow across the Himalayas from India and provide the Changtang the water essential for plant growth. At Pala's extremely high altitude, much of this falls in the form of snow, sleet, and hail.

Pala is located in the western Changtang, an area that is higher, drier and more severe climatically than the eastern portion. Sheep and goats, consequently, predominate in the west where grasses rarely get taller than a few inches, while yak are more abundant in the lusher eastern Changtang.

The western Changtang is one of the coldest and most inhospitable regions of the world, even though Pala, for example, is at the same latitude as New Orleans and Cairo. The reason for this is its altitude—the average altitude of the western Changtang being about 16,000 feet. Mean annual temperature drops roughly three degrees F for each 1,000 feet of altitude, so Pala's temperatures end up being like those of Alaska rather than New Orleans. The average temperature—the midpoint between the day's high and low—on the western Changtang is below 32 degrees F on more than 200 days in a year.

The Changtang, however, can be deceiving. Camped beside a glittering pristine lake with exotic waterfowl on a beautiful sunlit mid-summer day, the temperature in the sun can be 100 degrees F and the Changtang can seem an untouched paradise. But the reality of the Changtang is not the brief summer. Rather it is the bitter cold of fall which quickly dispels the warmth of August, dropping evening lows almost one degree Fahrenheit a night. By late September 1987, nighttime temperatures at the lowest (and warmest) of the Pala campsites (16,000 feet) were already in the low teens. And by late December, evening lows had dropped to minus 15-30 degrees F at this site, and were still decreasing. The effective temperature is even colder because of the wind chill factor—the western Changtang is exceptionally windy and sudden storm gusts can blow a rider off his horse or bury a traveler under drifts of freezing snow.

Diurnal variation (the difference between low and high temperatures in a single day), moreover, is huge. Noon temperatures of 35-40 degrees F frequently follow nighttime lows of -30 degrees F in the winter, and afternoon highs of 100 degrees F follow nighttime lows of 32 degrees F in the summer. From all points of view, the Changtang is one of the world's most extreme environments.

Birthing of sheep and goats is timed to occur in late winter/spring to ensure that when the kids and lambs are ready to be weaned, the new growth of summer vegetation is well underway.

Roughly two-thirds of the landmass of the Tibet Autonomous Region is covered by the valleys, plains, and mountains of the Changtang.

SUNLIGHT ON THE CHANGTANG

One of the delights of life on the Changtang is the abundance of sunshine, particularly during winter when precipitation is rare. Tibet is one of the sunniest spots on the planet, receiving about 3,400 hours of sunlight per year, according to Chinese scientists. The western Changtang epitomizes this feature. In the dead of winter when temperatures regularly dip to –40°F at night, the sun moderates the daytime cold, warming the tent and all within it, and making the shepherds' daily trek less onerous. For us, too, the sun was a precious gift we eagerly anticipated. No matter how cold the evening low, and no matter how difficult it was to summon the willpower to exchange the warmth of our sleeping bags for a seat near the fire in our frigid tent, the prospect of blue skies and shining sun in a few hours always made the cold less burdensome.

The Changtang's sunshine also allowed us to use solar energy to generate electricity for our equipment. We used an advanced "cardboard" solar panel. This turned out to be indestructible, despite repeated trampling by the nomad's livestock, which frequently showed up while the panels were staked out around our tent (see photo, p. 190).

The uplifting and warming sunshine of the high Tibetan plateau, however, also may have a down side. Tibet has one of the the highest prevalences of cataracts in the world, and many think this is caused by the intense ultraviolet radiation found at high altitudes.

(below) External poles and guylines give the black tents a spider-like appearance. These tents are sewn locally from long strips of woven yak-hair cloth about 15 inches wide. Each tent consists of two separate mirror-image halves that are connected at the top by two short lengths of rope and toggles that loop over a wooden cross pole supported by front and back wood pillars inside the tent. A long open space along the top allows smoke to disperse and can be closed with a flap when it snows.

(above) Following a fierce late-afternoon summer hail storm, a Changtang rainbow arches over a nomad camp.

(left) At 16,700 feet, the strong sun quickly melts the snow on the plains.

To Westerners, the life of the nomads seems exceptionally difficult. No matter how cold the weather, no matter if it is snowing, hailing or raining, the nomads must milk and herd their animals. Our image of the arduousness of life in Pala is epitomized by the vivid memory of several nomad women bent over at the waist milking their animals as a blowing snow squall deposited a cold white layer on their backs. But to the nomads, the unpredictability and ferocity of nature is a given. They accept hardship and discomfort as a matter of fact, a part of the natural way of things. Thus, on that day, as on every other day, the women simply kept on milking. While readily acknowledging the harsh climate and the bone-chilling cold, they do not share our perception of their way of life, and both men and women feel their way of life is far easier than that of farmers. A nomad neighbor named Phuntsog who was a father of four and owner of a large herd explained it this way:

> *Look, it is obvious that we have a very easy lifestyle. The grass grows by itself, the animals reproduce by themselves, they give milk and meat without our doing anything, so how can you say our way of life is hard? We don't have to dig up the earth to sow seeds nor do any of the other difficult and unpleasant tasks that the farmers do. And we have much leisure time. You can see for yourself that in the summer scores of farmers come here to work for us, but do we go to work for them? As I have told you several times, the farmers' lifestyle is difficult, not ours.*

Phuntsog's views reflect the deep conviction with which the nomads adhere to their customs and cherish their way of life. Although looked down upon by farmers and townsfolk in Tibet as simple, uncouth, and backward, and although they have little in the way of material possessions, the nomads are proud of their ability to live on the Changtang and wrest from it a way of life that they view as leisurely. These tough, quiet people have an air of dignity and contentment that is difficult for outsiders (even other Tibetans) to reconcile with their arduous life and relative poverty of possessions. The nomads see themselves as masters of the environment; but this is a mastery fundamentally different from that which we know in the West, or even that understood by farmers in Tibet. One middle-aged friend eloquently expressed the strange combination of awe, respect and confidence that the nomads hold for the Changtang:

The nomads twist huge hanks of wool into long skeins which are easier to store and transport.

At wool cutting, one or two nomads work inside a corral preparing the animals for shearing by tying their feet together. The trussed sheep are left at the feet of the shearers who pull the new ones toward them as they finish, generally throwing a leg over the sheep's neck to hold it still.

> *We build no canals to irrigate pastures here, nor do we fence and sow our pastures with grass seeds to enhance yields. They tried to make us do this during the Cultural Revolution, but that is not our way of doing things. The Changtang is a ferocious place—wait, you will see for yourself. One minute the air is calm and the sun is shining, the next it is hailing. It is not possible to try to control and alter the Changtang. We do not try—instead we use our knowledge to adjust to it.*

Shearing is normally done jointly by all the families in a camp, the object being to finish quickly since the shearing process disrupts the animals' normal pattern of grazing. Each family's wool, however, is kept separate.

The nomads' mastery, therefore, consists of developing strategies to accommodate to the vagaries of the environment—not to alter or transform it. Though they feel they are completely vulnerable to the climate and environment, they are also confident that their traditional way of life allows them to survive the worst of nature's catastrophes.

Another facet of their self-image emerged on a quiet mid-August afternoon when we joined a group of six men and youths who were seated in front of a corral shearing their sheep. As we weighed the wool, we inquired about wool prices and, by extrapolation, the nomads' subsistence economy. Pemba, an old and wizened nomad, suddenly offered an interesting answer to our queries about how he and his fellow *drokba* see their way of life. "You see," he said, pointing to the pile of wool at his side, "we live off the products of our animals. Every year our sheep provide wool, skins, meat, milk and butter which we use for food and clothes as well as for bartering with villagers to obtain barley, tea and so forth. And then every year virtually every adult female sheep gives us a new lamb. The same is true of our goats. So long as we can guide our animals to where there is grass, they take care of all our needs. They are our true provider and our measure of wealth—if they flourish, so do we."

This self-effacing understatement of their own role is one of the salient features of the nomads' world view. They typically describe their role passively, as simply letting the livestock follow their instincts, but we found that their subsistence economy is actually sophisticated, and that they are continuously monitoring conditions and responding to whatever impediments nature places in their way. These nomadic pastoralists, in fact, had a remarkable animal management system that balanced livestock and pastures, allowing them to inhabit the Changtang for centuries without destroying their resource base.

At the heart of that traditional system was their political position during the period before the Dalai Lama's 1959 flight into exile in India and China's assumption of direct administrative control over Tibet.

HISTORICAL BACKGROUND

The history of Chinese-Tibetan relations is complex, each country's position differing depending on what period over the past 1,200 years is under discussion. Matters are further complicated because these relations were never governed by formal treaties or agreements that spelled out the rights and obligations of each side. Not surprisingly, when the status of Tibet became a major international issue after the fall of the Manchu (Ch'ing) Dynasty in China in 1911, both sides expressed diametrically opposite views of the past. Whereas the new leaders of Republican and Nationalist China insisted that Tibet was an integral part of China, the Tibetans argued that their relationship with China had been that of "priest" and "patron," the Manchu Emperors of China being lay patrons of the Dalai Lamas and Tibet, and that Tibet had always operated under its own rulers, officials, language and laws. This is not the forum to explore the merits of these claims and counterclaims, and it will suffice to say that while Tibet was loosely subordinate to China for several hundred years prior to 1911, between then and 1951, it functioned as a *de facto* independent political entity, although it never received *de jure* international recognition of an independent legal status separate from China.

Wildlife is still relatively abundant on the western Changtang. Here the rare Tibetan black-necked crane flies off while sheep quietly graze in the background.

The Nationalist Government of Chiang Kai-shek never agreed to this *de facto* independent status for Tibet, and throughout the 1911-51 period sought to assert various forms of Chinese control over it. But China was weak and did not succeed until the Chinese communists of Mao Zedung came to power in October 1949. A brief invasion of Eastern Tibet in October 1950 encircled and captured a large Tibetan defending force of about 10,000, together with one of Tibet's four Cabinet Ministers who was serving there as Governor-General. With Tibet's best force destroyed and the road to Lhasa virtually open, the new People's Republic of China quickly succeeded in compelling a reluctant Tibetan government to accept a "17 Point Agreement for the Peaceful Liberation of Tibet." This Agreement left the old politico-economic system (including the Dalai Lama) intact in exchange for Tibet's formal acknowledgement of Chinese sovereignty over Tibet. The terms of this arrangement continued more or less in effect until 1959 when the Dalai Lama feared that the autonomy guaranteed in the 17 Point Agreement could not be maintained and fled into exile in India together with about 100,000 of his followers. From then on, China assumed complete and direct control. The traditional society had come to an end in Tibet.

This scene could have been described by a 19th-century explorer, so unchanged is the nomads' basic technology.

NOMADS, LORDS AND ESTATES IN THE TRADITIONAL SOCIETY

We spent numerous hours sipping butter-tea in smoky tents talking to elderly nomads about the "old society" as they now refer to the traditional period before 1959. Trinley, the 63-year-old nomad mentioned earlier, was one of our best sources for this topic.

> In the old society, we nomads of Pala were part of a large political entity (estate/fief) called Lagyab lhojang that consisted of 10 contiguous nomad groups belonging to (His Holiness) the Panchen Lama. The Panchen Lama owned all the pasture areas here and appointed officials from among us (the nomads) to oversee conflicts and collect taxes. He was our lord, although he never came here himself. I have never seen him... but we were under his rule.

The Panchen Lama was one of Tibet's greatest incarnations or incarnate lamas, second in stature only to the Dalai Lama himself. Tibetans, as Buddhists, adhere to the view that all sentient beings are part of a process of repeated reincarnation that spans eons and eons, but they go further than other Buddhists in believing that it is possible to identify the specific person who is the reincarnation of a great spiritual leader. They maintain that after the death of an incumbent incarnation, his "essence" selects a fetus to emanate or reincarnate into, this child being the new incarnate lama. The incumbent's followers search for this individual, guided by signs, portents, prophecies, as well as by tests that certify authenticity.

Once a spiritual leader is designated as an incarnation, his incarnation line continues over time—the current Dalai Lama, for example, is the 14th in his line of incarnations, and the Panchen Lama who died in 1989 was 10th in his. The property of incarnate lamas is passed down from incumbent to incumbent and accumulates over the centuries, the most famous incarnations becoming extremely wealthy and powerful. The Panchen Lama headed a huge fiefdom that had its own monk and aristocratic officials and controlled numerous farming and nomad estates (like *Lagyab lhojang*), whole districts, and thousands of subjects.

Yaks are used to transport all sorts of belongings, including infants too heavy to carry but too young to walk long distances. The cocoon-like bundle on the right yak is a young child.

The nomads of Pala, therefore, were the subjects of a religious lord, the Panchen Lama, to whom they paid taxes and provided corvee labor services. Their lord appointed the top officials in the area who, in turn, were responsible for maintaining law and order. Disputes that could not be settled on the local level were taken to the lord and his higher officials and, in theory, could ultimately be brought to the central government (headed by the Dalai Lama) if the lord could not satisfactorily adjudicate them.

The nomad families in *Lagyab lhojang* owned their herds, managing and disposing of them as they wished. But they were not free to leave the estate and move with their livestock to the estate of another lord, even if that lord welcomed them. They were hereditarily bound to Pala *(Lagyab lhojang)* and to their lord. If a situation arose where a family felt compelled to take its livestock and flee to a new lord (for example, due to a dispute with the lord's officials), the receiving lord would normally have to negotiate a payment to the original lord to compensate for the loss.

The feudal-like "estate" system present in *Lagyab lhojang* paralleled that found in Tibet's agricultural areas, both existing to ensure that religious and aristocratic elites (and the government itself) had a secure labor force to exploit the land they controlled. In essence, all land ultimately belonged to the central government in Lhasa, but over the centuries, segments of it had been granted to aristocratic families, great incarnate lamas, and monasteries for their upkeep and support.[5] Since land alone, be it agricultural farm land or pastoral grassland, was not a means of support without the presence of laborers to work it, the Tibetan system made things easy for lords by attaching laborers to these land grants, in essence granting the lord an estate or fief much like the manorial estates of medieval Europe, Tzarist Russia, and feudal Japan.

Being "bound" to the estate of a lord, however, did not mean that one could never leave one's village or encampment. So long as the obligations to one's lord were fulfilled, and families could hire others to accomplish this, members of the household were free to go where they liked, including visits, trading trips, or pilgrimages. Lords were interested in maintaining the flow of goods from their estates, not in micro-managing the daily lives of their subjects.

To be a subject ("serf"), moreover, did not imply poverty. Many of the Panchen Lama's subjects in *Lagyab lhojang* were wealthy, some owning very large herds of several thousand sheep and goats and many hundred yaks. Given this, it is not surprising to find that traditional nomad society contained important class distinctions. A stratum of poor nomads, for example, worked as full-time servants and hired laborers for wealthy nomads, even though both were subjects of the Panchen Lama.

The subjects of lords had rights as well as obligations, and so long as they fulfilled their obligations to the Panchen Lama, he could neither evict them nor refuse them access to his pastures. And although this was clearly no democracy, and could be oppressive when a lord and his officials were greedy, corrupt, and arrogant, generally the system was lax and the lord did not intrude into the nomads' daily lives.

Beneath the lord, the key institution in *Lagyab lhojang* was the family. Members of a family shared a tent, cooked and ate together, and jointly managed their herd, decisions being made by the family head. Sharing and cooperation within the family contrasted with a norm of fierce independence *between* families. The ideal for nomad families was to be self-contained units, and they preferred to hire individuals from the class of poor and indigent nomads rather than negotiating with neighbors to share tasks such as herding.

Authority in the family was (and is) generally exercised by parents. Respect for parents is strong, and Tibetan ideals hold that one should show gratitude to one's parents and obey their wishes; parents also normally control their family's activities—for example, where to pasture on a given day, which livestock to sell or slaughter, and even when and whom to marry. The story of Drolma's cancelled marriage is a poignant illustration:

When we returned to Pala in April 1988 after a few months stay in Lhasa, one of the first people we visited was our friend Norsam, a widower whose household included his 31-year-old daughter Drolma and two sons, one 20 and one 10 years old. As we caught up on events since our departure, we learned the sad news that Drolma's betrothal to a nomad from another group had been broken. While Drolma alternated between pumping the bellows, refilling our tea cups, and tossing handfuls of sheep- and goat-dung pellets on the fire, her father explained.

About a year before, a 35-year-old nomad from another district asked Norsam for permission to marry Drolma. She approved of the man, and her father, after considerable thought, also agreed to the marriage—but only on certain conditions.

Parents in Pala generally still arrange the marriages of their children, particularly their daughters. Normally, all daughters and all but one son leave their parents' household at marriage, so that the ideal family consists of parents, unmarried children, and one married son with his spouse and children. If parents have no son, they try to secure an "adoptive groom" for their daughter, that is to say, to find a male who will marry their daughter and join their household, adopting their name. However, there are no rigid rules regarding who marries out, and parents sometimes decide to keep a daughter in their household even when they have sons. In reality, they evaluate which of their children will take the best care of them as they grow old, and decide on that basis, rather than by following an unvarying "custom." In this case, Norsam decided to keep his daughter with him, and stipulated that the prospective groom had to move into his household and become his live-in adoptive groom. When we asked Norsam why he insisted on this when he still had two other unmarried sons living with him, he replied:

She is the best of my children —the one most likely to look after me well when I am no longer able to work... She obeys me; she never argues with me. She has real deep love for me ... My (20-year-old) son Shibum does not respect me well, and (10-year-old) Rinchen is too small for me to know how he will turn out.

Widebrimmed hats are much sought after because of the Changtang's intense sun.

The prospective groom, however, had other ideas. He was employed as a messenger at the Tsatsey district headquarters three days' ride south of Pala, and was looking for someone to live with him there. Accepting Norsam's terms would have meant living alone in Tsatsey most of the time and visiting Drolma occasionally while she remained with her father. He, therefore, countered with a proposal that Norsam shift to a base camp just

56

The first braid on either side of the face is strung with pieces of turquoise, coral, agate, and beads. Nomad women have 50 to 100 braids.

a day's horseback ride from Tsatsey where visiting would be easier. Norsam ultimately rejected this since he felt the change in the mix of grasses in the new area would harm his herd—and the groom responded by finding another bride.

Drolma abided by Norsam's decision, although she really wanted to marry the man. Had she defied her father and simply gone to marry him, no one would have stopped her, but her respect for her father was too strong. She could not bring herself to disregard his wishes—so she put his feelings ahead of her own. Although we felt sorry for Drolma, we found Norsam's assessment of the personalities of his offspring very astute and had to agree that in terms of his own welfare, Drolma seemed his best bet.

Parents, however, are not always able to enforce their will. Two years earlier, Norsam had given another son (three years older than Drolma) permission to marry if he brought the prospective bride to live in his household. A feisty single mother, she refused, informing Norsam's son that she would only marry him if he came to live in *her* camp, i.e., with *her* parents. The son, torn between the two, finally disregarded his father's wishes and went to live with the bride's family. The father and son hardly speak to one another anymore.

THE NOMAD ECONOMY AND THE CYCLE OF ANNUAL MIGRATION

The nomads' economy is, on one level, simple. Households raise sheep, goats, and yak under a "natural" system of pastoral production. Their livestock are not fed any specially sown fodder plants or grains, and survive exclusively by grazing on range forage.

This complete reliance on the natural vegetation, however, creates difficulties because the Changtang's high altitude permits only a single, short, growing season. In mid-September, the Changtang's grasses and sedges stop growing and lie dormant. Foliage at this time dries and turns color, cloaking the plains and mountains with a beautiful yellow-rust hue. This beauty, however, heralds the most dangerous phase of the annual cycle for the nomads' herds. New vegetation does not reappear until the following late April or early May, and even then is initially so meager that it does not play a large role in the animals' subsistence for another month.[6]

The consequence of this for their movement pattern is striking. Because there are no areas where the grass grows in winter, Pala nomads have no reason to migrate far in one year. Unlike nomads in Southwest Asia who typically move hundreds of miles in winter to lower regions where fresh grass is growing, Tibet's nomadic pastoralists cannot escape the harsh upland winter climate because all adjacent areas in Tibet have roughly the same single growing season. Their annual movement is only 10-40 miles. Indeed, they try to minimize travel, contending that it weakens livestock and increases mortality. As one nomad noted, why drive one's livestock on a long and tiring trek only to arrive at pastures no different from those available nearby?

Yak provide transport for heavy goods such as tents and are also relatively inexpensive riding animals.

Changtang livestock must forage for eight to nine months on dead plants left standing at the end of the growing season. The limiting factor is the amount of vegetation left at the end of summer, which must be sufficient to sustain livestock until the next year's growth begins. Dorje, a thoughtful old nomad, explained their perspective on this: "The animals can survive in summer (and fall)," he said, "even if the rainfall is poor, but unless there is enough grazing then for them to build up stores of fat, many will not survive the harsh winter eating the poor fodder."

To accomplish this, the Pala nomads move between two encampments—a main home-base three-season encampment used in winter, spring and summer, and a fall encampment. In late August or early to mid-September they make their major migration, leaving their home base for pasture areas usually one- to two-days' walk away which have been left ungrazed all season. The nomads reside at these fall encampments (which are re-occupied year after year) until late December when the forage is just about exhausted. Then they return with their sheep and goats to the original home-base encampment and use the remaining vegetation until the next growing season.

This seasonal migration pattern accomplishes just what Dorje said had to be done. It fosters the growth of the fat reserves the livestock need by providing abundant forage in the form of hay for the critical three months immediately preceding the onset of winter. In a sense, it extends the period of the good grazing season by three to four months. At the same time, the fall migration guarantees that a last cover of standing vegetation will be preserved at the home base for use during winter and spring.

(above) When they shift campsites, nomads pack some belongings in homespun wool sacks and some in net-like containers also made from wool. Still others, such as the yak hind-quarter, (below) are tied directly onto the yaks.

(opposite) Taking down a tent in preparation for the fall migration provides a good view of the tent's inner living space. The sitting room is the open area between the hearth in the center and the belongings that are piled along the outer edge.

This basic two-part migration system is only one aspect of the nomads' livestock management strategy. They also split their herds to take advantage of the different capacities and accommodate the different needs of their livestock. For example, only the sheep and goats leave the fall site and return to home base in December. The *dri* move to a series of different winter locations situated *higher* up in the mountains. There they establish satellite, or secondary, encampments called *kabrang*, staffed by family members or hired hands. The yak finally return to the home base five months later in May.

The reason for this became clear one April morning when we visited a young nomad friend camped with his yak at 17,500 feet, a full 1,500 feet higher than his main home-base campsite.

> *My camp is higher now because yak prefer* bang *(a type of sedge in the Kobresia family) which is most abundant along high slopes like these. Yak, unlike sheep and goats, are able to bite off grass and to lick/pull it up with their tongues. Thus, in winter they have no trouble consuming the low-lying* bang *(which is normally only one to one and a half inches high). And although it is much colder up here, the yaks are impervious to cold. Thus my parents stay at the home-base campsite with the sheep and goats, while I spend the winter here with the yak in our* kabrang *(satellite camp).*

The nomads also sometimes set aside a special pasture (or a section of the three-season location) for "birthing," and move pregnant sheep and goats there in spring when the lambs and kids are due.

Day-to-day assessment of local conditions also affects their movement. For example, in late spring 1988, vegetation became scarce around one home-base encampment and the three families moved their sheep and goats to a satellite camp one-and-a-half hours away. This saved the animals the energy expended on the daily three-hour roundtrip to the pasture, although it meant a daily two-hour roundtrip to the other side of the plain to fetch cooking and drinking water for the nomads themselves. This kind of micro-management based on local conditions works the other way as well. In the fall of 1987, one poor household headed by an elderly male skipped the arduous fall migration because the households at his home-base encampment agreed there was enough vegetation to sustain the additional grazing entailed by his remaining there. This practical empiricism characterizes the nomads' system of livestock management.

Finally, during the summer growing season, the nomads are careful to rotate livestock to different parts of the pasture area so that the vegetation regenerates (much like our lawns) for a number of days before another bout of grazing. Contrary to their unassuming comments that everything happens "naturally," the Pala nomads continuously observe and adjust to environmental conditions.

Another distinctive feature of the Pala nomads' way of life is the high value placed on remaining at their home-base encampment. This even has a special term: *shi-ma*. Although all the livestock move to the new pasture at the time of the fall migration, *not all the nomads accompany the herds.* Instead, a number prefer to remain at the home base.

The home-base encampment is located near one or more good sources of water and abundant vegetation for grazing, and is normally occupied for eight to nine months during winter-spring-summer. Households often shift their tents a few hundred yards once or twice during their stay at the home base to accommodate to the prevailing winds, but never more than a few hundred yards. There is no special order to the two to nine tents in an encampment; sometimes we found them side by side in a line, the guylines of one literally overlapping the next; in other instances they were more dispersed. We always found it interesting that living in this great empty wilderness where one can travel for entire days without ever seeing another soul or tent, the nomads preferred to pitch their tents literally overlapping each other. Even in the more dispersed camps, just several hundred yards typically separated the tents. Generally, each tent houses an entire family, but sometimes an elderly parent or a married child who is still part of the family will live next to the parents in his or her own tent, either eating at the main tent or having food brought from the main tent. Sometimes such individuals will join the main tent only for the main evening meal, making tea and *tsamba* themselves earlier in the day.

Since each nomad family expects to live in the same site year after year, the home-base site invariably contains a number of "improvements." For example, each household has a three- to four-foot-deep rectangular pit over which it pitches its tent in winter, and substantial stone or sod walls (windbreaks) surround these tent sites. These offer some protection from the relentless winds and bitter cold. The home base is also where wealthy households traditionally constructed small sod or mud-brick storehouses in which they kept their "possessions": carcasses, skins, and equipment such as ropes, saddles, and saddle bags. Nowadays some wealthy households construct small one-room or one-room-plus-storeroom dwellings, these being considered more comfortable in winter than tents.

Wooden pack frames obtained through barter with villagers are placed like a saddle on top of felt-backed pads providing an anchor for loads.

a winter tentsite with a sunken floor and windbreak

Nomads hire villagers in the summer to do many tasks they find unpleasant: constructing corrals, prayer-walls, houses, and storerooms, and tanning sheep and goat skins. Here villagers who traveled 20 to 30 days are building a stone house and storeroom for a nomad who has prospered under the new economic policy. These houses are seen as functional equivalents of tents and do not change their self-image.

When the nomads move their herds to a new site in fall, the actual move is amazingly simple. After the animals are milked in the morning, the herders immediately start off with the livestock for the new site. At the same time, other household members take down the tent, loading it on to male yaks that have been brought down from the mountains where they graze unsupervised until needed for transport. The various bags of grain, pots, churns, and so forth are tied onto a wooden yak saddle, a load being fastened by rope on each side, and one on top. A male yak can carry 100-200 pounds, so generally six to eight yak are plenty for a family. The entire operation from the start of taking the tent down to final departure takes one-and-a-half hours at most.

When a family's herds move to a pasture beyond the daily range of the home base, the family must also move with its tent (and belongings if they do not have a storeroom). However, the household head and his wife (or their elderly parents) often remain with the main yak-hair tent at the home base while their older children or hired shepherds take the livestock to the new pastures where a satellite camp is set up using either a smaller yak-hair tent or, more likely, a lightweight cloth "traveling" tent. Many households do not have enough members to simultaneously operate tents in two encampments, but the richer families generally maintain continual residence at the home base, hiring laborers to make up such deficits. They see it as the place with the most "conveniences." The short distances between home base and satellite campsites make this easily manageable since it is almost always possible to reach a satellite camp within one day on horseback. A single family, therefore, may have several separate camps and herds at one time—for example, in spring a yak satellite camp high in the mountains, a pregnant sheep-goat satellite camp on a specially set-aside "birthing" area, and a home-base camp.

This desire to remain at the home base does not conflict with or contradict these people's identity as *drokba*. Although *we* call them nomads or nomadic *pastoralists*, their own self-image focuses primarily on being complete pastoralists (i.e., practicing no farming) rather than on moving their herds (nomadism) or even living in tents. If they had houses at each of their pasture sites, or if they never had to move between encampments, they would not consider that in any way incompatible with their identity as *drokba*. We suspect that if they knew English they would have no objection to being classified as "ranchers," as the following incident illustrates.

In the winter of 1987 we were camped in a nomad traveling-style tent in a camp with both houses and tents. One friend, like many others, expressed concern for our well-being in this harsh and, for us, alien environment, and actually offered to move into his tent and lend us his much-prized new house, explaining that houses were warmer and reduced the incessant noise of the wind. When we refused, saying that we wanted to experience winter in a tent in the traditional nomad fashion, his face showed bewilderment and for days afterwards when he stopped by to visit, he reiterated how difficult it must be for us, and how much warmer and quieter it would be in his house. The other nomads in the encampment agreed completely with him and also advised us to move into his tiny one-room house. We finally realized that they did not share our image of *drokba* as "pastoralists living in tents." For them, pastoralism, not tent dwelling, was the key. Living in a house instead of a tent was a matter of comfort, not basic identity. The richest nomad during the traditional period had a house, and a number of the wealthy nomads had had storerooms, so having a house was actually perceived by them as a status symbol.

Rambunctious yak often buck off their loads. They are also prone to flick their horns, which these men are careful to hold while adjusting a loose load.

We should add that, like most of what the nomads told us about the environment, our friend's advice on houses was accurate. On some evenings, the roar of the wind was so loud in our tent that we were unable to hear the *Voice of America* shortwave broadcasts even with the radio held inches from our ears.

Notwithstanding their affinity for their home base and their view of a house at the home base as one of the ultimate luxury items, the nomads do move in order to subsist, always living in tents at the satellite camps and usually living in tents at the home base.

(pages 66–67) Summer grazing is essential for building the fat stores that enable livestock to survive the long and arduous winter when there is no new growth of vegetation.

PASTURE ALLOCATION AND RE-ALLOCATION

THE LONG-TERM VIABILITY OF all pastoral groups requires that their system of livestock management prevent overgrazing and destruction of their resource base—the vegetation. Critical to this endeavor is maintaining a balance between livestock numbers and the carrying capacity of the pastureland, and the nomads of *Lagyab lhojang* traditionally had an elaborate system of pasture re-allocation that accomplished this. The role of their lord, the Panchen Lama, is clearly seen here.

Traditionally, *Lagyab lhojang* was divided into thousands of named pastures of various sizes, often small, with delimited borders recorded in a register book. Although these pastures were not fenced off, boundaries were known by all and were enforced by the Panchen Lama's officials. Households received pastures proportionate to the number of animals owned, including multiple pastures appropriate for use in different seasons. Individual nomad households could use only the pastures allocated to them by the Panchen Lama's officials, even if they experienced drought or untimely snow. A nomad official explained:

> *Every pasture in our area and all the contiguous nomad areas in Western Tibet are named and allocated to some family (or small group of families) which has exclusive rights over it. While nomad custom allows us to use any group's pasture for one night while in transit, we cannot use such pasture areas for longer periods of time. This is as true of Pala today as it was during traditional times.*

Nomad families were completely independent of each other in terms of control over their pastures and animals. Thus, when we talked earlier of the nomads' migration to the fall camp, we meant more precisely each family's (or encampment's) move to its own fall pasture. There was no "common" pasture open to all. Ties between neighbors were weak unless they were kinsmen, and the backbone of the social and political system was the vertical link to the Panchen Lama, or today, the government. The nomad families of Pala, moreover, never joined together to form a single camp. The extent of this was strikingly revealed to us when we found that people living on one side of Pala could not identify children and youths in Polaroid photos taken on the other side. They simply had never seen them. However, when we explained who they were, they invariably knew of their existence and would say things like, "Oh yes. So that is what Dorje's son looks like."

Traditionally, each named pasture was considered suitable to support a fixed number of animals calculated on the basis of *marke,* a unit that literally refers to a weight of butter but was actually computed on the basis of the number of animals. One *marke* of pasture was suitable for use by 13 yak in the 1950s. One *marke* also equalled 78 sheep or 91 goats since seven goats or six sheep were calculated as the equivalent of one yak. In other words, a one-*marke* pasture would be assigned to a family with either 13 yak, 78 sheep, 91 goats, or some combination. A pasture with a two-*marke* rating would contain double that number, and so on.

Taxes were calculated on the basis of the number of *marke* assigned to a family. The main tax collected by the Panchen Lama was butter, followed by a potpourri of products such as: lamb skins, kid skins, salt, baking soda, money, wool, livestock (yaks and sheep), woven wool bags, and cloth, felt saddle pads and leather ropes. The nomads also had to barter large quantities of wool with the Panchen Lama at exchange rates that were often lower than the open market, and they were also responsible for delivering their taxes to one of the Panchen Lama's agricultural estates about a month's trek to the east.

Pala's traditional pastoral system balanced pastures and livestock by shifting pastures between families according to the results of a triennial household livestock census conducted by the lord and the local nomad officials. Families whose herds had increased were allocated additional pasture(s) and those whose herds had decreased lost pastures, the aim being to maintain only the specified number of animals on each pasture. Local fluctuations in herd size, therefore, were matched to the productive capacity of pastureland by: 1) shifting pasture areas every three years among families within a single nomad sub-group such as Pala; 2) shifting pasture areas among the Panchen Lama's 10 sub-groups in *Lagyab lhojang;* and in more extreme cases 3) moving entire households and their herds from one sub-group to another. Pastures (and taxes) remained fixed during the three-year interval between censuses.

The viability of this re-allocation system rested on the assumption that over a large area such as *Lagyab lhojang* and a relatively long period of time, disease and climatic disasters such as blizzards and drought create a "natural" (overall) balance between herd size and the carrying capacity of the pastureland. However, this "natural" culling of herd population does not operate evenly over a large area, wiping out equivalent numbers of livestock in each section. Instead, heavy losses tend to be very localized. For example, while some households in Pala in the spring of 1988 suffered 100% neonatal mortality of sheep and goats, their neighbors lost none or just a few percent. And in the summer of 1986, one area just west of Pala had five consecutive days of snow, losing about 30% of its herds since the animals could not get at the snow-covered grass, although Pala was unaffected. The snow prevented the nomads from moving to another area, making moot the legal question of their need to secure permission from another group to use their pastures. Thus, at any given time, some families and areas within *Lagyab lhojang* would have expanding herds while others' herds would be shrinking. Any single locality, therefore, might experience substantial sustained growth over time and potential overgrazing, even though losses in neighboring areas might keep the *average number* of animals unchanged and/or decreasing. So while climatic and disease factors probably precluded exponential growth of livestock *over the large area*, they would not prevent overgrazing on specific pastures unless the pattern of herd growth and decline on each pasture area was also accommodated. This, of course, is precisely what the traditional system of re-allocating pasture every three years accomplished. It conserved the resource base in specific localities by shifting pasture and herds to ensure that each pasture contained only the specified number of livestock. This system of re-allocation is no longer in effect—a point to which we shall return.

It is not unusual to come across a solitary tent, although more often 3 or 4 tents make up a campsite.

HORSES AND THE HAY-CUTTING TRIP

"A HORSE IS NOT A HORSE if it does not carry uphill, and a man is not a man if he does not walk downhill" goes a Tibetan saying. The nomads are extremely fond of their horses which are bred locally and, like most Central Asian horses, are quite small, not much bigger than ponies (approximately 47 inches at the shoulder and 49 inches long). But they are tough; as the saying indicates, their main job is to carry a rider uphill where the going is very difficult. Horses in Pala are a true luxury item, having no relevance to subsistence since Tibetans, unlike the nomads of Mongolia, do not milk mares, nor eat horse flesh, nor herd on horseback. They are also scarce—out of almost 9,000 head of livestock in Pala there are only 28 horses, and only 25% of Pala's households own a horse. Horses, therefore, command a high price. In 1987 one horse sold or traded for about five yak or 40-50 sheep, thus placing them out of reach of all but the middle- to upper-income households, particularly when one adds to this the need to supplement their diet with grain and

(below) Horses are luxury items that indicate a family's wealth. Their natural diet is normally supplemented with fodder, cooked grains, peas, and tea leaves.

hay and then the need to purchase saddles, stirrups and saddle rugs. The expenses for "tack" are substantial since nomads feel about horses much the way Americans feel about their cars, and there is real competition among horse owners to have beautiful saddle rugs and gear. For example, when we expressed our thanks to the nomads for all their help by making each household a present of a few Polaroid photographs, more often than not the male household head would spend hours rounding up and saddling his horse so that he could take a picture with it .

(above) Tibetan nomads pay great attention to horse tack. Colorful matching woven rugs come in sets of two, one placed under the saddle and the other on top, creating a splash of color in the bleak environment. The Pala nomads, who do not weave rugs, obtain these from other areas in Tibet, and nowadays, even from Tibetan refugee factories in Nepal and India.

Because horses are not nearly as hardy as the nomads' other livestock (and because they are worth so much), they are given more attention and expenditures than their other livestock. For example, they are usually covered with a blanket when they are let out to graze in winter and spring and are commonly fed grain supplements of approximately one-and-a-half pounds per day (mixtures of boiled grain, leftover tea leaves and lentils). The only livestock to receive such treatment, they are also fed hay obtained annually from a special pasture that is left ungrazed throughout the growing season.

(left) Horses are protected from the bitter sub-zero winter cold by woolen blankets woven locally.

Once a year, on a government-designated day in September, nomads from Pala and several adjacent areas travel 3 or 4 days to a pasture area that has been left ungrazed all year to cut hay for their horses. In 1988 about 100 tents attended.

The nomads cut grass from early morning until evening, taking a two-hour midday break.

Hay cutting commences on a specific date in mid-September set by the government (or by the lord in the "old society") and at a specific location at the intersection of three nomad districts. By this time, the wool has been shorn and the grass-growing season is at an end. Nomads, mostly men, from the three adjacent districts (Tsatsey, Tshochen, and Nakdzang) are involved. Some of these, like those from Pala, travel three to four days to reach the site. In 1987, word was transmitted to all nomad encampments by letter and oral message about two weeks before the starting date. The nomads had been anticipating this date and immediately set about finalizing preparations for the trip—how many and which yaks to take, and who to send with them. Some nomads shared tents with friends or relatives, thus messages went back and forth between households to arrange whose tent, whose tea churn, whose pots and pans to bring and when to depart.

As soon as we arrived we understood why this was the "hay-cutting" area, for unlike the rest of *Lagyab lhojang*, it consisted primarily of tall vegetation (about one to one-and-a-half feet) thick enough to be gathered into a handful and cut with a sickle. We counted just over 100 tents and were amazed at the activity there. In contrast to the few people and the slow pace of life at a nomad encampment, the grass-cutting camp was bustling with activity—some taking their horses and yak out to graze, others talking and joking with friends they had not seen for a year or more. The bazaar-like atmosphere was enhanced by a dozen or so traders, some nomads, and others, villagers from weeks away. Even the government store opened a temporary branch. They all sat behind heaps of miscellaneous wares including everything from prayer books and rosaries to wooden saddles and bowls, to pots and ladles and plastic jerry cans to Chinese "boom boxes" used to play prayer chants and traditional melodies typically on cassettes imported from Nepal (e.g. see photo, p. 162).

At 8 a.m. on the specified day, an official blew a whistle to start the cutting. Everyone rushed to the adjacent slopes and plains in search of the "perfect" spot. People would cut for an hour or so, stuffing handfuls of grass into their cloaks, then pause to fashion them into two-foot-long twists and carry bundles of these back to their tent to dry. Then they returned to start all over again. In the evening, attention focused on the traders and their wares, the nomads making the rounds of the 10 or more "stalls" set out on blankets on the ground, examining goods, asking prices, and bartering energetically. When darkness made business impossible, other activities began: some younger nomads danced and sang, others played Tibetan dice or ma jong, while most just sat around drinking tea and talking. The festive atmosphere was contagious and we had a steady stream of nomads from other areas who wanted to see and chat with the *chigye* (foreigners) who spoke Tibetan. Scores of nomads now know that U.S. astronauts walked on the moon and that it is evening in American when it is daytime on the Changtang. For us it was a wonderful opportunity to talk with nomads from adjacent districts about their conditions.

The hay-cutting gathering is not all work. Some traders also come to sell all sorts of items from prayer books to candles and from cooking pots to Chinese-made radios. And in the evening, men and women dance and sing traditional tunes until the wee hours.

The impact of hay cutting on the overall pastoral economy, however, is slight since this area provides too little hay to accommodate livestock during those times when snow prevents the animals from grazing, let alone for general use as a food supplement in winter and spring. And although some is occasionally given to lactating sheep and goats, virtually all is used to supplement the winter diet of the horses owned by the more affluent households. And nowadays, each nomad household also has to provide a small hay allotment to the district officials for their horses. Poor nomads go to cut grass to sell to the richer households who want more hay than they can cut (or who were unable to come at all that year). This is one of the ways that the poor supplement the insufficient income from their small herds.

The flurry of activity is short-lived. As soon as a nomad household has cut enough hay to load their yak, they break camp and leave. Five days after the tent city materialized out of nothing, the plains again were empty—and stay so until the following September when the cycle of nomadic pastoral life will again bring 100 or more tents to this obscure spot on the Changtang.

LIVESTOCK IN THE PASTORAL ECONOMY

COMPLETE ECONOMIC DEPENDENCE ON LIVESTOCK is the feature distinguishing the *drokba's* way of life from that of villagers. Livestock products directly provide food, clothing and shelter, and indirectly (through trade) yield grain, tea, ironware, and manufactured goods such as sneakers, aluminum pots, and clothing.

The yak is the quintessential Changtang animal: cold and high-altitude adapted. Surprisingly, the nomads' generic term for yak is not yak at all but *nor*—a word that normally translates as "wealth." The term yak is actually reserved for only the male *nor*[7] while female nor are called *dri*.

The yak is unique to the Tibetan plateau and surrounding areas. Its thick outer coat of coarse hair, soft undercoat of cashmere-like wool, and subcutaneous fat layer prevent heat loss and permit it to live year-round in the open. We have seen them grazing at 18,000 feet in winter in areas where the temperature regularly drops to –40 degrees and –50 degrees F at night. Indeed, the well-adapted yak does not thrive in warmer temperatures at altitudes much below 10,000 feet.

Adult male yak weigh between 440-550 pounds, and are about four feet tall at the shoulder and four-and-a-half feet long. Females are 20-25% smaller. The Tibetan yak provides "heavy transportation": it is extremely powerful and has great endurance even at the highest altitudes. It is the only animal that can carry the nomads' heavy and bulky black tents, each side of which weighs about 100 pounds, and do so through snow and crossing passes at 20,000 feet and higher. Yaks can also be saddled and ridden, and function as a kind of poor-man's horse. Although they have quite a comfortable gait, they are slow compared to horses and we found them somewhat difficult to steer because the reins are strung through their nose hole rather than attached to a bit.

Male yak are the only livestock that are left untended in high mountain valleys where they graze by themselves. They usually do not wander too far from where they are left, so when they are needed for transportation, it is not difficult to locate and bring them back. *Dri*, on the other hand, are herded on a daily basis like sheep and goats.

Since our research required interviewing and examining the nomads in all of the various home-base and satellite encampments, we frequently traveled with yak. Normally, the nomad we hired to move us would get the yak the day before our departure and tie them up on a tether line overnight to ensure that they would be there first thing in the morning. However, our traveling plans were delayed several times when the yak were not found where they were last left, and had to be searched for in the adjacent valleys. The first time this happened, the nomads told us that even though the yak hadn't arrived that evening, they would certainly get there early the next morning so we would still be able to depart by 10–11 o'clock. When we awoke the next morning to find the weather clear and sunny, we decided to save some time by taking down our tent and packing in anticipation of the arrival of our yak. But nine o'clock and ten o'clock passed with no sign of the yak. Then the unpredictable Changtang weather decided to highlight our poor judgment by first clouding over and then raining, forcing us to put up our tent and unpack in the midst of the storm. Our 15 yak finally arrived at 4 p.m., the drenched herder explaining that the yak had moved farther than normal and that he did not immediately find them. We never again broke our camp until we saw the carrying yak with our own eyes (or at least through our binoculars).

Sheep begin reproducing in their third year and do so annually thereafter.

Yak provide food, shelter, and clothing for the nomads. Their coarse belly hair is spun and woven into tent material, and their soft cashmere-like wool (called *kulu*) is used for ropes and blankets. Their hide is used for the soles of boots and, of course, yak provide large quantities of meat, as much as 175-275 pounds from an adult male. In addition, the females provide relatively large quantities of milk throughout the year.

A single yak is worth much more than a single sheep or goat —roughly six sheep and seven goats traditionally were bartered for one yak. However, because of the amount and quality of the vegetation available in Pala, yak comprise just 12% of the Pala nomads' livestock, and are not as important for the overall economy as sheep.

Tibetan Changtang sheep have adapted to life at high altitude with more hemoglobin and larger lungs than lowland sheep, as well as a dense and long coat of wool. They too provide meat, milk, wool, and the skins needed for the nomads' winter clothing. They are also used for transporting goods: adult males can carry 20-30 pounds of grain or salt in a saddlebag similar to that used for backpacking dogs in the U.S. There is also a lively trade in the animals themselves, the nomads exchanging sheep with villagers for grain and goods, and to pay them for work such as tanning skins.

Goats thrive in this area. Like the sheep, they have higher hemoglobin, more red cells, and breathe four-five times faster than their low-altitude relatives. They provide more milk than sheep and for longer, and their skins are used for the nomads' heavy winter clothing. Traditionally, they were less valuable than sheep because there was no market for their hair or cashmere and little for their meat since villagers prefer mutton. Recently, however, their economic value has skyrocketed as a consequence of the emergence of a thriving national and international market for cashmere (discussed below).

The availability and quality of animal products vary throughout the year, and the nomads' traditional production strategy has accommodated to this by: 1) converting temporary abundances into storable forms that can be used throughout the year; and by 2) collecting products at peak quality. Dairy products exemplify the first strategy; meat, wool, and cashmere the second.

Yak are saddled and used for riding. They have a smooth gait but are relatively difficult to steer because the reins are strung through their nose rather than attached to a bit.

(right) Dri give milk all year round.

The fresh butter is ladled out of the churn and set aside until enough butter accumulates to be sewn into a sheep's stomach where it can be stored for as long as a year.

DAIRY PRODUCTS

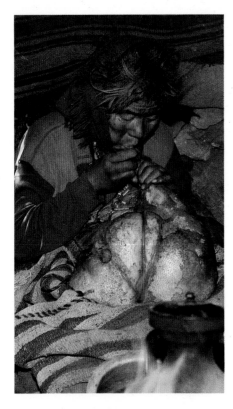

Sheep, goats, and yak give different amounts of milk and for different lengths of time. Wanam explained the essence of his dairy production:

You have to understand that although our yak, sheep and goats all provide milk, the sheep and goats do so for only part of the year (sheep for three months and goats for four-and-a-half months in summer). Only the dri *(female yak) give milk year round. Thus, while I get lots of milk from my animals in summer, I get very little in winter.*

We measured the milk from his 155 milking goats/sheep and 11 female yak, and found that he gets about seven gallons a day at peak yield in mid-summer when all three are giving milk, but only about three quarts a day in winter.

So we drokba *transform a large portion of the summer milk abundance into butter and cheese since these can be stored and utilized later when the fresh milk is insufficient for our needs. They can also be sold whenever we need other products.*

The nomads, consequently, consume virtually no milk *per se*. Instead, they first make yogurt the same way we do by bringing milk to a boil, cooling it somewhat, adding a "starter" and letting it sit covered overnight. By the following mid-morning they have a rich, tart, and smooth yogurt called *sho*. The women churn most of it into butter, setting aside a portion for the day's meals. Households with large herds usually keep the yak *(dri)* milk separate because it yields the yellow butter that is preferred to the white butter of sheep and goat milk, but most simply mix all their milk together.

In winter, when families get only a small amount of milk, the large wooden butter churn is replaced by a skin churn made from a sheep's stomach. Yogurt is poured into the inflated stomach and shaken.

(below) Butter forms after about an hour's churning

An hour or so of lifting and plunging a wooden paddle in a chest-high wooden churn, about 12 inches in diameter standing alongside the tent, produces butter. In wintertime, when very little milk is obtained, two- to three-days' worth of yogurt may be saved to process at one time, and churning is usually done in the tent in a container made from a sheep's stomach. The churner blows air into the stomach to inflate it, pours in the yogurt, and then shakes it back and forth on her lap until the butter forms. The resultant butter, which is about 6.5% of the weight of yogurt, is sewn tightly into sheaths made from sheep's stomachs where it stays fresh for about a year, enabling the nomads to spread the caloric value of their dairy products to the seasons when milk is scarce.

After the butter is removed from the yogurt, the leftover liquid ("buttermilk") is boiled and strained to yield a cheese that, when fresh, resembles crumbly white farmer's cheese. This represents another 23% of the weight of the yogurt. A little cheese is consumed fresh, but most is sun-dried into rock-hard bits and stored for use in winter and spring. Cloths spread with drying cheese are a common summer sight, attracting birds, cats, dogs and children, all hoping to sneak a tasty morsel. Dry cheese lasts for years. We still have cheese from 1985 in perfect condition.

The liquid left after the cheese is removed, the whey, is sometimes consumed by the nomads, regularly fed to the dogs, and boiled to make the women's black make-up (döja).

(above) The day's fresh white cheese is spread onto a cloth to dry in the sun. It takes 4 to 5 days of sunny weather to convert the crumbly soft cheese into rock-hard dried bits. In the foreground is partially dried cheese from the previous day.

(right) Very young girls like to imitate grownups by wearing makeup—but need help with application.

Döja is made by boiling whey until it becomes a dark and thick concentrate. Some of this is applied immediately (with a small tuft of wool) while the rest is stored in a can or wood box. A single batch of *döja* can last for weeks or even months. Reusing it is simple. A few drops of water are added to the thick concentrate which is then reheated at the edge of the fire. As many of the photographs in this book illustrate, *döja* is carefully applied by women on their forehead, nose and cheeks with a small tuft of wool. Men do not use it at all. Nomads generally say that it protects the skin against the sun, but it actually is used more as a cosmetic to enhance beauty. Young girls start applying it around 10 or 12 years of age and continue to do so until their 40s and more rarely, 50s, and it is most frequently applied by women who are concerned with appearance, e.g. single girls of marriageable age and newly married women. Like their counterparts in the U.S., women put it on when they want to look particularly attractive. For example, on several occasions we saw women whose husbands were expected to return that evening from a long trip wash, braid their hair, and put on fresh *döja*.

The nomads' make-up covers the cheeks, temples, and brow ridges. Made by boiling whey in a small bowl until it blackens and thickens, it is stored and reheated before use by placing it in the coals of a fire.

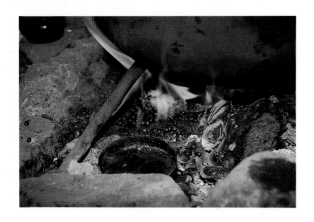

(right) applying make-up with tufts of wool, peering into a shiny brass mirror

Although the nomads typically say their way of life is easy because livestock provide all their needs for them, pastoral production really takes time, work and skill. Obtaining and processing milk exemplifies this. It is almost exclusively the responsibility of women who milk the animals, make the yogurt, and churn the valuable butter. In summer (June through August), when sheep and goats are milked twice a day, the yield per animal is highest, and the largest number of animals are giving milk daily, dairy work may require six hours. Starting shortly after daylight, the adult and teenage women emerge from their tents carrying wooden pails and ropes of braided yak hair to begin the sheep milking. As her companions keep the herd swirling slowly about her, one woman grabs her animals by the horns and pulls them one by one, each facing the opposite direction, and loops a section of the rope over the neck in a crochet-fashion slip knot. This creates a long line that looks like two long interdigitating lines of animals facing each other. Each animal is held fast by a single long rope tying it to its neighbors facing the opposite direction.

Once the animals are securely tied face-to-face, the milkers rinse their hands and start milking. This method of tying the animals immobilizes them in a line-up for an hour or two while the milkers work their way down the line, usually twice, each milking only her own animals (which are tied next to each other) bending at the waist and reaching the udder from the back. Separate households may herd together but almost always keep their milk separate. After milking is finished, a woman pulls the loose end of the rope tying the animals and the "slip-knot" unravels the row of crocheting to free the animals at once. The process is then repeated with the goats.

(above) A woman returns to her tent with a full milk pail in one hand and a butter churn borrowed from her mother in the other. One son is balancing a spatula of coals from his grandmother's fire which his mother will use to start her own.

Milking the *dri* is a bit more complicated. The one- to three-year-old calves are tied every evening, the wooden peg worn on a string around their necks fastened to a loop on a tether line pegged into the ground. This prevents them from suckling and keeps their free-ranging mothers from wandering too far during the night. In the morning, the *dri* are rounded up and, one at a time, hobbled with a short rope around their forefeet. The milker then unties its calf which races to its mother. It is allowed to drink for a moment to start the milk flowing, and is then dragged away and retied. After milking, the calf is untied and allowed to forage with the mother all day.

After several hours of milking and an hour or so of churning, there is a midday pause of about five to six hours when other chores are done, including preparing *tsamba*, fetching water, spinning and weaving wool and making yogurt. The evening milking session for sheep and goats (but not *dri*) lasts an hour or two, ending usually after sunset. From October to May, only the morning milking of the *dri* has to be done.

Milking time, however, is not all work. Usually several families at an encampment tie their animals together in a single lineup and the women of the camp gossip and laugh while each milks her own animals. Milking invariably also brings out their children who play alongside the animals as if on a playground.

Some play at being animals, walking on all fours holding discarded yak horns in their hands, while others make believe they are antelope, hopping around holding pairs of elegant antelope horns to their forehead. Older siblings may race around carrying babies piggyback, or putting them down to practice tottering to mother and back. Those learning to talk are encouraged to do so. One little girl, coached by her mother and sisters, learned to say "Cynthia" very well, giggling delightedly as she did so. Others practice counting by enumerating the animals in line.

(opposite) The nomads use an ingenious method of tying sheep and goats for milking. Two long interdigitating lines are made by tying the animals head to head with a crochet-like knot looped over and around each animal's neck. After milking, the end of the rope is pulled and the entire line unravels.

(right) Children will play with whatever is at hand, including sets of antelope horns.

(above) This 78-year-old woman quickly finishes milking her few animals but stays around relaxing in the sun and chatting with other milkers and children.

(left) Nomad children who wake up after their mothers have gone out to milk may run around camp naked for a while until she or someone else helps them to dress.

92

Children often try to "help" the milkers in sweet and humorous ways, one trying to push back a sheep that has turned out of line, another slapping a rump, while another earnestly holds the end of the rope tying the animals head to head. The nomads are exceptionally affectionate and loving with their children and many of the tender moments we witnessed took place at this time. One tranquil summer evening Nyima gave a ladle to her five-year-old daughter who had been imitating her by tugging at the udder of the next animal in line. The girl, now with a milk container just like mom, diligently, though without any skill or much success, "milked" the goat for a few minutes and then carefully balanced the ladle on our scale so we could weigh the milk, just as we did for the adults. Then she poured her few drops into her mother's wooden pail, receiving a big hug and kiss for her effort.

Children amuse themselves even when the weather is freezing.

Winter satellite camps are established for yak in the higher mountains so that they can graze on a type of sedge they relish. This young woman's father and younger brother remained with the sheep and goats at their home-base campsite 1,500 feet lower.

Since women normally do all of the milking, churning, cooking, and collecting of dung fuel and water, our first summer with the nomads seemed to confirm the widespread urban Tibetan stereotype that women do all the work in nomad society while the men sit around "relaxing." When we asked the nomad women whether they sometimes resented the men's lack of help in the milking cycle, many could hardly understand our question, so alien was it to their view of a "natural" division of labor. Nyima, who has seven children and a large herd to care for, one day responded to our suggestion of inequality and oppression with an air of incredulity. "But of course I don't resent having to do the milking and my other tasks. The men have their work to do as well and I wouldn't want to change with them. I'm always here by my children and tent and do not have to undergo the hardship of long-distance travel as the men do when they go on their journey to collect salt from distant lakes, or when they go to trade in winter with villagers a month away."

At first we found this hard to believe, but the more we traveled among the nomad campsites, Nyima's attitude became somewhat more understandable. When nomads travel they continue regardless of the weather: neither rain, nor snow, nor hail compels them to change their plans—they load up and move on with their animals until they reach their destination. Walking with them all day in blizzard-like conditions, and watching them repeatedly load and unload the rambunctious yak, wearing no gloves, yet tying and untying knots in sub-zero temperatures, we gained appreciation for the women's point of view which sees their division of labor as complementary rather than exploitive. And in fact, some men occasionally do help out with "women's" tasks such as churning and even milking if their household is shorthanded or the woman is sick.

The men, similarly, accept their role as travelers and traders, despite the hardships and dangers involved. The same men who lounged around the encampment while the women milked, and did not think to help with many of the daily tasks, were always ready to load up some yaks, saddle a horse, and travel to another campsite a day or two away for even minor reasons, oblivious to snow, hail, or rain.

The first time we moved with the nomads we did not realize this and told them we would like to leave the next morning if it were not raining. This brought only blank stares which we perceived as meaningful only in retrospect. Sure enough, the next day we awoke to find it raining. As we lingered over breakfast tea in our dripping tent, the nomads walked up with the yak all saddled, ready for us to break camp, load up, and move out. We had no choice but to do so, and later simply adopted their tactics. The unpredictability of the Changtang's weather actually made this reasonable since it is likely to change from rain to sun, and then perhaps to hail or snow, and back to sun over the course of a single day.

MEAT PRODUCTION

Just as summer is the time of dairy plenty, winter is the time of meat abundance. Most households slaughter a sheep or goat in late August to celebrate completion of the wool shearing, but almost all other meat is harvested all at once at the start of winter. One old nomad neighbor of ours explained the reasoning behind this:

> We kill now because this is the optimum time. The good summer and fall grass has helped the animals build up the stores of fat that give the meat its good taste, and the animals have not yet started the inevitable winter-spring loss of weight.

The nomads think of their livestock as capital. At worst, they try to draw on the interest alone, using only the yield of annually recurring animal products and "spending" (bartering or slaughtering) no more livestock than reproduction replaces. Ideally, they try to increase the capital fund by selling or slaughtering fewer head of livestock than are added to the herd through birth. Disaster for the nomads occurs when high mortality confronts a family with the need to eat or sell off part of its capital to survive, knowing full well that this could start a downward spiral ending in impoverishment. Neonatal mortality is particularly insidious because it reduces the flow of new females into the herd and thereby threatens the ability of the herd to replenish itself. Nomads typically try to preserve their capital when this happens by temporarily working for others to meet basic subsistence needs. This reduces their need to sell and slaughter livestock and gives them hope that the inherent capacity of their goats and sheep to reproduce quickly—newborn female kids and lambs begin to reproduce annually in their third year—will allow them to restore their capital level (their herd) after a few good years.

The annual winter slaughter is the time when such decisions occur, and therefore the time when the future composition of the herd is determined. It is, therefore, one of the junctures at which the family head's experience, skill, and values come to the fore. The nomads can do nothing about herd mortality which is a chance element in their production system, but they can control the composition of their herd by deciding which (and how many) animals to cull each year.

While non-reproductive animals are slaughtered first, even barren females and old males are valuable because they yield wool and hair annually, can be used for transportation, and are a source of meat. They will not be culled if a household's meat needs are already met or if the overall herd size cannot sustain the loss. Because of this, the number of animals slaughtered for food varies with the wealth of the household—the more animals a family has per person, the more it can sell or kill without cutting into its capital. Thus, while the average number of sheep/goats killed for meat per person was 4.4 in 1986 through '88, the richest families slaughtered about eight to ten animals per person and the poorest only one to two per person. About nine percent of the total livestock in Pala was culled for meat in 1987.

Most people tend to think of "native" peoples living in remote locales such as Pala as being homogeneous—as sharing identical values and attitudes. Nothing could be further from the truth in Pala. While these nomads all shared something we can call Tibetan nomad culture, like us they have very different personalities and values. This is very striking with regard to their attitudes toward herd management. Some are eager to acquire the symbols of success and status (for example, silver flint strikers, new shirts made from colorful Hawaiian-style cloth, a horse, saddle rugs, tape cassette recorder, and so forth), and are willing to trade or kill extra livestock to obtain these immediately, even though it cuts into their herd capital. They assume the reproductive power of their herd will make this up the next year. Others are more interested in increasing their herd capital. They are willing to defer gratification, preferring to wear a torn shirt an extra season over trading a sheep for a new one. They speak disparagingly of the nomads who are highly concerned with conspicuous consumption, while those who like the good things in life ridicule the affluent conservatives for living poorly despite their wealth. Most nomads agree with those who forego luxuries today to build wealth for the long-term, but the differences are as significant as they are among ourselves.

Once the decision is made about which animals to slaughter, the killing is generally completed over the span of a few days. Most nomads, however, do not physically do their own slaughtering because killing brings bad *karma*. As Buddhists, they believe that reincarnation is determined by one's *karma*, i.e., by the balance of merit (good deeds) and demerit (bad deeds). So they avoid the demerit that goes to the person who actually does the killing by hiring other nomads to do this. Traditionally, these were either from a small category of "polluted" nomads or were simply poor nomads who needed the wages. They performed this and other "unclean" tasks such as castrations and ear-brand cuttings.

Killing is done in a manner that conserves the blood for use in sausages. Sheep and goats are killed by inserting a long (3–5″) sewing needle between two vertebrae in the neck, while the yak are killed with a sword. Because of their size, killing a yak requires the cooperation of several nomad men who first must lasso the animal, pull it to the ground, and bind its four legs together. A brief prayer is said for the "soul" of the yak (upper left photo) and then a sword about two feet long is inserted into the stomach and slowly thrust upwards to penetrate the heart. It is left there, or moved back and forth, for about 10 minutes until the animal dies (middle left photo). Once an animal is dead, the males of the household are free to help in the actual butchering—the sin being only the act of killing. The entire animal, even the head, is boiled and ultimately eaten, although except for the sausages, the meat is not processed in any way before storing. Carcasses are simply piled up along the sides of the tent or in the storehouse until they are needed. On several occasions in winter when we leaned back in a nomad tent we found to our surprise that our backs and hands were resting on a sheep or goat head.

The strength of these values was brought home to us vividly once when we were out of meat in Wanam's encampment. With 1,000 sheep and goats in front of us, we had to wait two days until one could be slaughtered. Wanam, reciting prayers with his rosary, explained to us, "I will of course sell you a prime sheep, but right now there is no one in our encampment (of three tents) who slaughters. I will send a message to the camp on the other side of the lake and ask Dorje to come and kill the sheep."

Slaughtering the animals in late November/December not only ensures that each animal yields the maximum calories, but also enables storage without spoilage. December's cold and aridity freeze the carcasses whole—there is no need for special processing such as slicing or drying or smoking. Sometimes the inner core of a large hunk of meat such as a rump of yak does not completely freeze, but it remains unspoiled until at least the following June when the warmer weather initiates deterioration. For most families summer spoilage is not a great problem since their supply of meat is usually exhausted by then.

Slaughtering just once a year, however, creates a storage problem. A household of five (the average size in Pala) will average 22 carcasses, heads, skins, and so forth to store, while a rich household may have about 45-50 carcasses to deal with. Not surprisingly, these nomads have always had a strong desire for storerooms.

OTHER LIVESTOCK PRODUCTS: WOOL, HAIR, SKINS, AND ANIMALS

The nomads' herds provide more than meat and dairy products. Sheep yield wool for weaving and barter, skins for clothes, stomachs into which butter is churned and sewn for storage, and intestines, organs and blood for sausages. The animals themselves are valuable trade items. In 1987, one sheep sold for about 50-75 pounds of barley (roughly two- to three months' supply for one adult). A pound of wool, the principal marketable sheep product, brought the nomads about six pounds of barley in 1987. Since Tibetan sheep are sheared once a year (in late July) and yield about one pound per animal, the wool from roughly 45 sheep provide enough grain for one adult's subsistence for a year. Wool is spun into thread and then used for weaving cloth and sewing. It is also used to make felt, to braid ropes, and even to place on wounds.

Each encampment selects an auspicious day for shearing by consulting the traditional Tibetan lunar calendar published nowadays in book form by the Tibetan (Traditional) Medical College in Lhasa. It not only indicates the extra days that are included (or deleted) to make the 360-day lunar cycle (30 days per 12 month) keep par with the actual change of seasons, but also the auspicious and dangerous days as calculated by Buddhist astrology. Households cooperate and/or hire shearers to complete the work in a single day since this simplifies the logistics. This is a happy time for the nomads, analogous to farmers' harvests, as it represents the culmination of a year of husbanding their sheep. They slaughter an animal at this time and enjoy rice and unusual foods, for example, *tü*. This is a rich mixture of mostly butter, cheese, molasses, and *tsamba* that resembles stiff cookie dough in texture.

The wool that the nomads keep for their own use must first be spun with a wooden spindle, a ubiquitous fall and winter activity. They do this in their spare moments—in their tents, while walking with the herds, and even while traveling. Different types of spindles—obtained through barter—are used to obtain different thicknesses of thread. A backstrap loom is used by women to weave bags, clothes, or belt fabric.

Animal fleeces are as essential as meat because they are sewn into the nomad's basic garment, the *lokbar*. *Lokbar* resemble a long-sleeved, belted robe with the full fleece facing inside and the waterproof hide on the outside. They are worn ground-length by women and hitched up to the knee by men, and are extremely heavy. Adults' *lokbar* are usually made from 10 tanned adult sheep or goat skins and weigh twenty to twenty-two pounds. Children's *lokbar* are also heavy; a seven-year-old's *lokbar*, for example, weighs six to eight pounds. Men do the actual cutting and hand stitching of the garments, tailoring being one way men supplement their income. The outside of the women's *lokbar* is decorated with eight to ten horizontal stripes of brilliantly colored felt sewn onto the skin. Men's *lokbar* have a single black stripe at the hem of the skirt and the sleeves. The sleeves of the *lokbar* are cut to hang eight to ten inches below the hand, functioning like gloves when the hand is not being used. *Lokbar* double as blankets at night, the nomads curling up inside them. In winter, some men also wear sheep or goat-skin trousers (with the fleece on the inside), although most wear heavy wool trousers woven by the nomad women.

There is a constant need for skins to make new garments since the efficiency of these *lokbar* decreases as the fleece wears thin. Ideally, one should have a new *lokbar* every three to four years, but it is difficult for poor families to sustain this, and one of the indicators of poverty in Pala is the need to wear old and worn *lokbar* in winter and spring. Old *lokbar*, however, are not thrown away. They are fine for summer and fall when the weather is less severe, and are used for many more years like this. And adult *lokbar* may be cut down and remade into children's *lokbar*.

Thirty to forty lamb and kid skins make a luxury summer version of the same garment that weighs only half as much. These are in short supply since no nomad would think of deliberately killing his kids and lambs for their skins, and their availability depends on natural mortality. Lamb and kid skins (with their fleece) are also used for the standard men's and women's winter hat, although more wealthy males usually have fox-skin hats.

(opposite) The family head guards the door of his corral complex to prevent his herd of yak from fleeing while their cashmere-like undercoat is being combed out. The glare of sunlight off the snow at high altitude makes snow-blindness a serious threat; protective coverings have been used for centuries. Before darkened glass was available, the nomads cut slits into leather. This nomad was suffering from a bad case of conjunctivitis and was using his new factory-made goggles to keep out dirt and cut down the glare. The inroads made by recent changes is seen in his ingenious adaptation of Chinese sneakers—he has sewn the traditional Tibetan boot leggings onto the top of the sneakers. This way he can tie them by the customary boot strap rather than by shoelaces; it's also warmer.

(above) The man at the right takes a head census by counting each sheep as it is released from the corral.

Considering the importance of skins to the nomads' survival, it seems curious that they do not tan their own skins. They regard tanning as work fit for farmers, whom they call *pöda,* a social category they consider fundamentally different from themselves. In 1987 they paid farmers one live sheep for every 10 skins tanned. Every May, after the plowing is completed in the farming areas, teams of villagers fill the trails, moving north to nomad country where they work and/or trade with the nomads. Every generation one of two of these villagers (who are actually semi-nomads in the sense that while they have fields, they also maintain herds of livestock) marries a nomad girl, stays, and becomes a nomad himself. The opposite, however, does not occur—nomad women do not marry into farming villages, mainly because they have no experience and skill in any of the essential farming work that village women must do. In early September, the trails fill up with villagers making the month-long return trip home for the harvest. This time, however, they are driving flocks of sheep and goats—their earnings for the long summer of work.

Goats were considered less valuable than sheep in the past because there was no market for goat's hair (in contrast to wool) or *kulu* (cashmere), and little market for goat meat. But goats are more hardy than sheep and are considered to provide some insurance against losing an entire herd in a very bad year. Goats also give milk for six to eight weeks longer than sheep and give more milk per day, and their skins are generally considered to be warmer than sheep skins. The value of goats, moreover, has increased dramatically over the past three to four years as a result of the development of a lucrative international market for cashmere.

*(above) Yak, like goats, have kulu.
However, the nomads either have to lasso
and truss the yaks or drive them into
corrals to control them and safely obtain
cashmere.*

*(opposite, above) Felt is made by wetting
and patting down wool (and/or goat hair),
rolling it tight in a blanket, and pounding
it. After this process is repeated a number
of times, the wool coalesces into felt and is
peeled off the blanket.*

*(opposite, below) Cashmere (kulu) is now
one of the nomads' most valuable trade
items. It is combed out from goats the
same way Americans comb the soft
down undercoat from long-haired dogs.*

Cashmere is the soft down or undercoat of goats. It is analogous to
the soft hair Americans comb out of their long-haired dogs after winter.
Like us, nomads use combs with long teeth to obtain this *kulu*. We found it
astonishing to see them sitting in the dirt, combing out this unattractive
undercoat, knowing that it might end up in Bloomingdales as a $400
sweater. The nomads make no terminological distinction between goat's
kulu and the soft undercoat of yak (and dogs and antelopes). Yak *kulu*,
however, has little economic value since the legal definition of cashmere in
the West restricts it to the *kulu* of goats. Thus, whereas one pound of goat's
kulu brings 29 pounds of barley, the same amount of yak *kulu* brings only
about four pounds.

The nomads obtain, on the average, only about a quarter pound of
cashmere per goat, but the high value of cashmere products has made the
economic value of goats equivalent to that of sheep. Since the price of
cashmere is rising much faster than wool, goats may well end up the basis
of a new affluence for the nomads. This is already being reflected in herd
composition. Whereas there were three sheep for every two goats in 1981,
in 1988 the ratio was one to one.

HERDERS AND DAILY HERDING

HERDING HAS TO BE DONE 365 DAYS OF THE YEAR. With no store of fodder to distribute to their livestock, the nomads must take their animals out to graze every single day. Because of the complex way they divide up their livestock into separate grazing herds, one of the constant problems facing families is a shortage of herders. For example, since *dri* are always herded separately, as are lactating sheep and goats, and a regional category of adult males, non-lactating females, and nursing infants, each family frequently operates three sub-herds and needs three herders virtually *every day of the year.* Most households don't have enough people, so make a variety of other arrangements including cooperating with neighbors and hiring shepherds.

Nowadays it is common for several households in an encampment to pool their animals and share the work involved in taking them out to graze. If three grazing herds are needed for a while and there are three households, a typical cooperative agreement would have each household supplying one herder and for each of the three herds to include all three households' livestock. Each nomad family cuts one ear of its sheep and goats in a distinctive way to guarantee unambiguous identification when herds are mixed. This is done when the animals are a few months old and, like butchering, is considered a polluting activity. Animals are also marked with an orange dye to indicate ownership.

Because cooperation requires reaching mutual agreement on many issues such as which herd goes where, many rich households prefer to avoid potential conflict by controlling their herding. They supplement their own labor by hiring one or two herders for a season, or even for a year, paying nowadays one sheep per month of work plus food and sometimes a set of clothing.

Separated by the 17,500-foot Parongla Pass from the main portion of Pala, this subsection of Pala, known as Bünsum, is located beside Lake Shuru.

Within a family, herding is done by both sexes and by adults and children beginning as young as eight or nine years of age. It is a low-prestige job for adults, however, and is typically done by teenagers and low-status adults such as unmarried siblings and daughters-in-law without children. The household head selects the herders and instructs them where to take their flock each day. Herders generally work for four to five days in a row and then have a day off, someone else in the family filling in for them. But a variety of arrangements accommodates the different mixes of people (and personalities) in households. For example, in one household we knew well, a brother and sister aged 10 and 23, respectively, alternated every two days. In another, cousins from two cooperating families alternated days.

Work as a herder is at the same time trivial and crucial to the nomads. It is trivial in the sense that little to no skill is required to herd adequately, and children 8 to 10 do an acceptable job because the complex decision —where to go on any given day with the herd—is made in advance by adults.

The shepherd is responsible for directing the feeding of the flock, moving it so that it grazes evenly over an area, and more important, preventing the flock from scattering, since stray sheep and goats are easy prey for wolves and other carnivores. Although this requires no special skill—really just staying awake and watchful—when it is not done properly, disaster can occur. For example, during the summer of 1987 a 34-year-old shepherdess fell asleep and awoke to find her herd nowhere in sight. When she finally tracked down the animals, she found that four had been killed by wolves. One of her brothers was so furious with her that he punched her, knocking her down.

Although herding is low prestige for adults, young children often see their first selection as a herder as a sign of maturation. One 11-year-old boy who began to herd *dri* during the summer of 1987 used to beam when his father put his enormous cowboy-style hat on the boy's head and sent him off. But herding, on the whole, is uncomfortable and boring.

Herders work a long day, usually leaving about mid-morning and returning only in the evening. The herder is usually alone all day, has no hot food or drink, and no protection against the elements, which in summer include rain, sleet, and hail, and in winter include bitterly cold temperatures and ferocious winds. Some herders relate that on the coldest winter days when the sky is overcast, they can't speak when they return in the evening because their faces are too stiff from the cold, and can't open the tent door because their hands are too numb to work the wooden toggle that fastens the tent-flap.

(left) *A goat licks her newborn kid.*

(below) *Weak or small babies obtain extra nourishment by suckling from a female whose baby has died. The mothers have to be held or else they will not tolerate this.*

The most critical work for the herder occurs at lambing. Lambs and kids are born in early spring when temperatures are extremely low and the tiny, wet newborn lamb or kid is at high risk of freezing. The herders' responsibility is to see that this does not happen. They are expected to keep track of all females about due to give birth so that they can intervene immediately and dry off the newborn baby by rubbing it with dirt. Mistakes at this time can cause high neonatal mortality and prevent increases in herd size. Not surprisingly, young children are considered unreliable and too easily distracted to be useful, so adults, even the head of the household (or his wife), will herd during these months.

(above) *The shepherd dries the wet newborn kid by rubbing it with dirt. He then puts it in the striped sack on his back and carries it all day since kids cannot keep up with the herd until they are a few weeks old.*

112

We went out with a goatherd on a bitterly cold and windy early April day to see how this operated. Before we set out, the 17-year-old herder identified a goat that was about to give birth. She would not stay with the herd, wandering off 100-200 yards by herself, and, as the time for birth approached, searching for a convenient depression in the ground in which to lie down. She often vanished while we were distracted by something in the rest of the herd, and several times we had to search around to find where she was hiding. When she finally gave birth, the herder was right there. He let her lick her kid for about 20 seconds, and then gently took the kid from the mother and dried it off. Since infant kids can not keep up with the herd, he put it into a wool sack on his back and carried it around for the rest of the day.

During birthing, the herder's role is equally important at night. The pregnant females are kept in open corrals and the herder has to sleep with them in order to be there to dry off the newborns immediately.

After birth, the nomads continue to protect their capital by keeping the babies at night in specially constructed bins of clay or rocks or sod. We measured one bin which was roughly five feet long by two feet deep by four feet high and contained 10–15 newborn lambs. The bins are covered at night with woolen blankets or pieces of sod and functioning to cut out the wind and conserve the animals' own body heat and keep them warm.

CARNIVORES AND PREDATION

Wolves are found in Pala and pose a continuing threat to the nomads' livestock. Every year they attack and kill sheep and goats, yak, and horses. Lynx and snow leopards also occasionally kill livestock, but it is the wolves who cause the most harm. The nomads talk about this danger frequently but can do little to control them. They keep guard dogs that roam loose at night in an attempt to scare predators off, but they do not have the modern rifles they would need to hunt them; putting out poison or baited traps is as likely to kill their own dogs and livestock as the predators.

After wolves killed several female yak during the spring of 1988, the local Pala officials set a small bounty on killing wolves, and persuaded a group of nomads to track the wolves from their most recent kill. After several days of searching, the nomads finally located the wolves' den on a craggy face high in the mountains. Leaving their dogs on the plains, they climbed up the precarious slope and killed the four wolf pups they found. However, while they were doing this, the adult wolves circled down onto the plains and killed two of their hunting dogs. The hunters later discovered a second den and killed those pups too, but their success was tempered by the loss of the dogs.

DIET

THE PALA NOMADS REAP LIVESTOCK PRODUCTS to provide the food they need to survive. But their diet is highly unusual in that they consume vastly different diets during winter and summer, eat no fruits and virtually no vegetables. Nor do they utilize all the potential foods around them. For example, they do not eat fish or fowl, even though many live beside lakes teeming with fish and migratory ducks and geese. They do not eat carnivores or rabbits or the abundant wild ass, which they classify as a horse because of its non-cloven hoof. They explain this simply as due to their cultural heritage—that *drokba* do not eat those foods.

Nomads eat two or three meals a day. Some families have tea, either alone, or with *tsamba* or leftovers, before starting the morning's milking; others have nothing until after milking when all families have a mid-day meal of tea with *tsamba* and sometimes yogurt or leftovers. This meal may be substantial in winter when it is likely to include meat. Herders eat before leaving camp around mid-morning, some taking food to eat during the day, but most do not eat until they return. All families eat their main meal in late evening after the milking is done and the animals are settled in for the night. In summer, supper is often *tsamba* plus a thin stew consisting of a little *tsamba* and animal fat, and perhaps some dried radish. In winter, the evening meal is usually a substantial stew with lots of meat and *tsamba* or boiled flour dumplings. The nomads explain that the heavy stew helps keep them warm during the bitterly cold winter nights, and there is some scientific evidence from the Andes that such stews are actually effective. They drink Tibetan-style tea, flavored with salt and butter, throughout the day, often with a little *tsamba* if they are hungry.

MEASURING THE NOMADS DIET

In order to find out how much and what people eat, we weighed an entire day's intake for each person in a household on about 20 occasions over the year. This meant one of us sat in a tent from the time the first person awoke until they went to sleep and weighed everything they ate and drank. The nomads got into the spirit of the work and helped out. For example, if we were distracted momentarily, the diner would put his bowl on the scale to catch our attention before taking a mouthful.

Just 15 foods plus tea comprise virtually the entire nomad diet. These are dairy products (yogurt, milk, cream, cheese, buttermilk and whey), meat products (animal fat, blood and meat including organ meat), barley (*tsamba*), wheat flour, rice, cooking oil and very rarely dried radish and dried cabbage.

Men eat twice as many calories as women during the summer and fall and about 40% more during winter. Similarly, boys eat more than girls. These sex differences are found in most societies and are explained by males' larger body size, higher basal metabolic rate and greater muscle mass. There is also a striking seasonal difference: caloric intakes were two to four times higher in winter than summer. This is primarily attributable to a huge increase in the con-

sumption of animal fat and meat after the late fall slaughter. Women aged 15-59 showed the largest seasonal difference, eating almost four times as many calories in the winter as in the summer and fall.

Tsamba, obtained by trading animal products for barley, is the dietary staple, contributing roughly half to three-fourths of the calories in summer/fall and one-fourth to one-half in winter. Adults consume an estimated 175 pounds of *tsamba* per year and children (aged 5–14) 160 pounds. Some flour and rice are also consumed. Dairy products contributed a higher proportion of total calories in summer when milk production is high and absolute caloric intake is lower (15–25% in summer vs. 5% in winter). In winter, milk production is low and they are obtaining many calories from meat.

Tibetan-style tea flavored with butter and salt contributes a few percent of total caloric intake while

contributing most of the added salt, although the winter stews contribute salt too. Adult men consume a median of 7.3 to 10.7 grams of salt a day in addition to that occurring naturally in the foods themselves. Women consume less additional salt because they eat less food and children consume very little salt indeed, mainly because they drink little tea.

Curious onlookers watch Cynthia Beall measure a nomad woman in the authors' Lhasa-made tent. Such measurements provide information on nutritional status.

THE SALT TREK

SINCE TIME IMMEMORIAL, TIBETAN NOMAD MEN have been the main source of salt for the villagers and townspeople of Tibet and the adjacent Himalayan kingdoms of Nepal, Bhutan, and Sikkim. Each spring Pala men drive transport animals 140 miles northwest to salt flats at Lake Drabye, a 50- to 60-day roundtrip. Goats and sheep are normally used, each animal carrying a load of 20-30 pounds. Yak can carry much heavier loads but most nomads have relatively few male yak and can transport larger amounts of salt using the more numerous sheep and goats.

From a distance, the salt flat at Drabye looks like a vast white snowfield, and even up close, it crunches underfoot, crystalline—like crusted snow. It was hard to accept that this white substance was really salt until we each picked up a piece of the white crystal from the surface and tasted it. The salt, about a foot deep, appears to be replenished in summer when, according to the nomads, the dry salt bed is covered by a foot of brackish water.

Like so many of the nomads' tasks, the entire process of gathering the salt has been worked out to the last detail. One nomad we met at the lake explained how they do it:

> On the trip to the lake we go very leisurely so that our animals can maintain their strength. Pasture is a problem, for the new growth of spring grass has yet to begin and we must depend on the grass left over from last summer. At the lake, pasture is even more sparse than along the route, since there are so many nomads and animals concentrated there. Because of this, we send an advance team of four or five men to dig up and pack the salt. Then when we arrive with the animals, we can load up immediately and leave the next day.

Nomads pitch camp right on the salt flat as they collect salt for their own use and sale.

The advance team pitches its tent right on the salt. One or two men pound the crust with yak or sheep horns to break the salt into small pieces, while another scoops it into wool saddle-bags, and a fourth sews the saddle-bags shut and piles them to one side. The day before the pack animals arrive, a corral is made from bricks of salt and the filled saddle bags are piled beside it.

The sheep and goats are driven into the corral, 30-40 at a time, and the back-breaking job of loading begins. Several nomads stand at the entrance to the corral to prevent animals from escaping, while a couple of others, often singing haunting work songs, wade into the densely packed throng, grabbing an animal by its horns and dragging it to a man at the entrance. He takes over, wrestling the animal's head and pinning it between his legs, fixing the saddle-bag in place, and tying it on firmly. The animals, however, are continually trying to break loose and the men are soon sweat drenched and panting from the effort to keep the thrashing animals under control. Compared to the preceding days' slow and steady salt pounding and filling bags, the loading process is lively and noisy.

By evening, the sheep and goats are loaded and settle down to sleep right on the salt, their saddle-bags not to be removed until they reach Pala a month later. One advantage of using sheep and goats for transport is that they relieve the nomads of the time-consuming task of loading and unloading scores of animals *each* day. When they leave for home early the next morning, the main group of transport animals has spent less than one day at the salt flat itself.

Each pair of salt bags weighs about 20 to 30 pounds.

The Changtang's salt flats have always provided a free source of income for those willing to make the trip. Old Sonam explained the importance of the salt trip for him some 40 years ago.

Back then I was a poor bachelor without a family (or livestock). I survived by working for rich nomads—herding, cutting wool, and so forth. I also earned substantial income every year by going to collect salt. We drokba have a saying, 'The salt lakes of the north are a storehouse of precious gems; whosoever's hand is longer can reach and take them.' And this is true. Although I did not have transport animals of my own, there were always wealthy nomads who did not want to take the long and arduous trip themselves and were willing to hire poor people like me to accompany their animals. In fact, I used to enjoy the trip despite its hardships. Ten to 20 of us would travel together taking along the best food—good mutton and lots of butter. We stopped early every day because the animals had to graze, so we had lots of time to sit around the fire enjoying each other's company—talking, joking and eating during the long evenings.

Wearing a fox-fur hat and a prayer amulet around his neck, a young nomad prepares to fill empty woolen salt bags.

He then related another traditional saying regarding the trip to collect salt:

For the best man, it is a place for playing (i.e., easy)
For the middle-quality man, it is a place for singing (i.e., singing work songs meaning it is like work)
For the inferior man, it is a place where you shit in your pants! (i.e., because you have to work so hard)

Collecting the salt, however, and getting it home are just the first stages of the process. Selling it requires another long caravan trip to the areas of the farming villages about a month to the south. The nomads make this trip to barter salt for grain the following fall or winter, soon after the villagers have completed their harvest. All told, therefore, collecting and selling the salt require an investment of roughly three to four months for both the nomads and their transport animals.

(above) In the division of labor, usually one nomad is responsible for sewing the salt bags closed.

(right) The first step in obtaining salt from the salt flats is to pound the crust and break the salt into bits.

(far right) Tying the salt bag on the sheep is hard work as the nomad holds the animal steady by keeping its head between his legs, slips on the bag, and secures it firmly under the tail and around the neck.

(opposite) In order to maximize the amount of salt each sheep and goat will carry, the nomads tamp the salt vigorously into the locally woven bags.

After the nomads return home, some of their salt journeys onward. Other traders purchase and carry it still farther south until some ultimately crosses the Himalayas and reaches Hindu villagers hundreds of miles south of the Changtang. For example, when Goldstein conducted research with Tibetan villagers in Northwest Nepal, he commonly encountered Hindus from central Nepal who had come to buy salt from the Nepalese Tibetans who, in turn, had bought it from the Changtang nomads.

(left) The first step in loading sheep is getting them into a corral.

(below) Once the sheep and goat loads are tied, the animals are not unloaded until they arrive in Pala several weeks later. This spares the nomads the time-consuming daily task of loading and unloading hundreds of animals.

Recently, the government has made dirt roads leading to many of the main salt flats in Western Tibet, and has started hauling salt from the lakes in trucks. Cheaper ocean salt also now competes with Tibetan rock salt. These changes have decreased, but not eliminated, the market for the nomads' salt. Many Himalayan and Tibetan villagers still prefer the taste of Tibetan salt, and since the nomads obtain the salt at no cost, even a modest exchange such as the 1987 rate of five units of salt for four units of barley is still profitable.

Nevertheless, very few Pala nomads took the trip in 1987. Most did not feel the profit was worth spending four months on the trail, particularly since the poor forage at this time of the year could impair the health of their livestock, possibly producing increased mortality. Salt collection, therefore, is an option in the nomads' system of production whose utilization varies depending on the overall well being of the nomads. If economic conditions are bad, then more households will want to make the trip. If they are relatively good, fewer will take the trouble.

HUNTING

ANOTHER "OPTIONAL" FACET of the nomad economy is hunting. The Changtang traditionally abounded with wild antelope, blue sheep (*bharal*), Marco Polo sheep, wild asses, gazelles, and wild yak. Between 1959 and the mid-1980s, local officials and army personnel are said to have killed large numbers of these animals for meat by hunting in jeeps with modern rifles. More recently, a lucrative trade in antelope skins has developed. The antelope's soft "cashmere" (*kulu*) undercoat is combed out and smuggled to India where it is used to make the finest shawls. There is also pressure on small carnivores such as the snow leopard and the Tibetan lynx, both of whose pelts appear to end up as Russian-style fur hats.

Recent laws prohibit this type of hunting, and the Chinese government has cracked down somewhat on the illegal antelope-pelt trade, but each day dozens of leopard and lynx pelts are offered for sale in the Lhasa market, and many more never reach the market because they are collected directly by traders scouring the Changtang for pelts. The price in Lhasa's open market for the beautiful tawny lynx pelts has more than doubled over the past two years, bringing about 800-1000 *yuan* (the equivalent in value of two to three yaks) in 1987-88.

Despite all this, wildlife is still abundant in Pala and other parts of West Tibet. As we traveled between encampments and to areas surrounding Pala, we regularly saw herds of wild asses, antelope and gazelle, some as large as 100 animals.

(below, and opposite) Pelts of endangered animals such as the Tibetan snow leopard, fox, and Himalayan tiger are regularly available in the Lhasa marketplace, although officially there are laws prohibiting killing them.

Nomads brace their matchlocks on gun rests made from antelope horns or wood.

The nomads traditionally hunted the blue sheep, wild yak, gazelle and antelope, and still maintain that tradition. One of the best hunters in Pala is Damdrin, a taciturn 44-year-old bachelor who lives alone. He explained the nomads' hunting technique when we accompanied him on a hunting trip in search of the blue sheep or *na*, as the nomads call it.

I always travel with my hunting dogs and rifle so that if I spot some na I can go after them. But you've seen my matchlock rifle. To begin with it is only accurate up to 30–40 meters. Moreover, it takes a very long time to fire. Even though I keep my rifle loaded with powder and a lead musket ball [held in the barrel by a wad of wool plugging the muzzle hole], after I spot a blue sheep I still have to plant the gun on the ground with its gun-rest, then light the wick with a spark from my flint-striker and then put the wick to the small powder bowl on the outside of the gun. This in turn ignites the powder in the barrel and fires the bullet. By the time I have done all that, the prey is long gone. With just our Tibetan rifle we are no match for the na. That is why we always hunt with our hunting dogs. They tilt the odds in our favor. As you will see, as soon as I spot blue sheep on a mountain slope I turn loose my dogs. Their job is to corner one of the na among the crags, and bark loudly to lead me to the spot. The best dogs will even try to run back a ways to make it easier for me to find them, all the time, of course, keeping their prey at bay. Once I get there, I have plenty of time to set up my rifle and shoot. In fact, during the commune period when I had no rifle, I climbed above the cornered na and heaved down large rocks to kill it.

(below) Two nomads set off to hunt the "blue sheep" (na), accompanied by their valuable hunting dogs.

These sleek *naki* or "blue sheep dogs" look like tawny-colored greyhounds. Bred for hunting, the best is worth a yak nowadays. They tend to be treated better than the nomads' watchdogs, and in some cases are treated almost like pets, given affection and allowed to come into their tents. Cats, on the other hand, are generally treated like pets—they are allowed inside the tent, are sometimes petted, and are even fed milk by rich families. The hunting dogs typically do little in camp but sleep. However, as soon as their owner-hunter heads out of camp, they immediately perk up and follow eagerly. Seeing them in action, we quickly understood why they are so valued. When Damdrin spotted a small herd of 10 blue sheep and released his three dogs, they took off like greyhounds, bounding up a steep, rocky slope whose base was just over 18,000 feet. They were quickly out of sight. We followed as best we could, moving toward their barking. Damdrin, who continually complained to us that he couldn't do strenuous work because his lungs were no good, went up the steep slope at a very fast pace without a single rest. We tried to keep up with him, following as quickly as we could. We were slowed, however, by poor footing on the 45-degree incline covered with loose dirt and rock, and by having to stop every few minutes to gasp for breath. It graphically demonstrated the difference between lowlanders acclimatized to living at high altitude and real native highlanders. Although life at 16,000-17,500 feet normally did not bother us greatly, we were no match for the nomads at strenuous work.

The nomads' hunting dogs, however, are ineffective against the antelope and gazelle which inhabit the open plains where they cannot be cornered. Instead, the nomads use two other methods: placing a simple snare along paths to watering holes and shooting from ambush. The latter involves hiding in a depression near a regular trail in the hope of getting off a shot. As unlikely as this may seem, in May 1988, two nomad friends hid like this from morning until nightfall (with a brief break for lunch) for three days until, on the last afternoon, each shot one antelope.

This hunting is not a serious threat to the antelope since only six to seven were killed in 1987-88. More seriously, in spring 1988 we met several nomads from another *shang* in Tsatsey who had came to Pala with a modern rifle they had borrowed from a Tsatsey official. Although officials have to account for all their bullets and these nomads had to obtain their own bullets, this was no problem. For example, they were on sale at the hay-cutting marts for two *yuan* a piece. These nomads were able to shoot six antelope in two weeks and were planning to move on to a new location.

(above) Some families have pet cats and allow them the run of their tents. This is not the case for dogs, with the exception of a few favorite hunting dogs.

(opposite) The snare is used at mating season, when many animals come together and use well-marked trails back and forth from the water hole. It is embedded just beneath the surface at the top of a hole 3-4 feet deep. Its main section is circular, made from horn that is soaked until pliable and then bent and covered with yarn spun from yak hair. Short horn prongs point inward and downward from the circle. The animal's foot enters the trap with no problem but cannot easily be pulled free because the prongs cut into its legs. However, these traps are actually pretty flimsy contraptions, and we believe the nomads when they say that they are not effective when used alone. Thus there is a backup. A length of strong rope about an inch in diameter woven from spun yak-hair is arranged in a slip knot—one end looped around the top of the trap and the other firmly embedded in the bottom of the hole under rocks and dirt. When the animal steps through the main snare, it steps into the slip knot too. As it pulls to get free of the prongs, the slip knot tightens, and even if the animal is able to break the prongs, it remains immobilized by the rope.

Not all nomads hunt. Some clearly enjoy the challenge of hunting, and others hunt because they like the extra meat, but many if not most Pala nomads have renounced it. Our friend Wanam explained, "We are Buddhists, and as such should not kill other creatures. Most nomads in Pala, therefore, are like myself and nowadays do not hunt. However, if we are desperate for food, we all will hunt. I myself did so to maintain my family during the Cultural Revolution when my wealth was confiscated and I was excluded from the commune. But these days I do not need game to survive and will not take the life of another sentient creature." Another young friend, who was an accomplished hunter with fine dogs in 1986, proudly informed us in 1987 when we asked to go hunting with him, "Over the winter I decided it was sinful to kill animals when I don't need the meat, so I gave away my rifle and no longer hunt. I think it will be better for me to say prayers than hunt."

This religious sentiment was reinforced by the sad experience of an old nomad neighbor of ours. He explained:

> Last summer some traders came and said they would pay high prices for lynx or snow leopard pelts. I wanted some extra money so last fall, after you returned to America, I bought two Chinese steel traps and baited them. I thought I was lucky when I was able to kill two snow leopards and sell them for 500 yuan (equivalent to the value of two young yaks). But during the winter, my wife suddenly fell ill and died. She was very healthy before this, and I now know that Dargo, our powerful Buddhist mountain-god protector, was angered by my slaughter of these animals for profit and showed his displeasure by taking my wife from me."

Since then, despite the enormous profit, trapping for pelts is no longer done near Mt. Dargo.

Hunting and salt collecting, therefore, represent non-essential components of the nomads' subsistence—they are economic reserves. In bad times more nomads turn to salt collection and hunting to supplement their income, while in good times most will not bother to make the three- to four-month effort needed to collect and sell salt, and will adhere more closely to Buddhist tenets by renouncing hunting.

a mother and her newborn lamb

a hunting dog

Pica live in burrows and compete with livestock for vegetation. Their burrows dot the plains and are a danger when riding since horses may step into them and stumble.

the antelope

(right) bar-headed geese

(below) Tibetan wild ass are abundant in Pala.

HIGH-ALTITUDE HYPOXIA

As many Colorado skiers, Himalayan trekkers, and Andean tourists know first hand, arriving abruptly at high altitude can be physically unpleasant. Common initial symptoms for lowlanders include headache, nausea, insomnia, and the inability to perform normal activities. Usually these symptoms abate after a few days. They are caused by high-altitude hypoxia resulting from lowered barometric pressure. Oxygen is the portion of air that supports life and comprises about 21% of air. At 5,000 meters (or 16,400 feet), an altitude within the range of the Pala encampments, the barometric pressure is nearly 45.5% lower than that found at sea level—422 torr vs. 760 torr. Similarly, nearly 45% fewer oxygen molecules enter our lungs with each breath, and thus fewer oxygen molecules diffuse into the blood for transport to the cells which must be continuously replenished with our most vital nutrient. Only 85% of the nomads' hemoglobin is actually carrying oxygen (versus over 95% at sea level). This is the hypoxic stress of high altitude.

However, high-altitude natives like the Pala nomads live without symptoms because they have adapted physiologically to their lifelong hypoxic stress by enhancing their ability to transport oxygen from air to tissues. The principal mechanism is an increase in the amount of hemoglobin in the blood which increases the blood's capacity to obtain oxygen from the inspired air in the lungs.

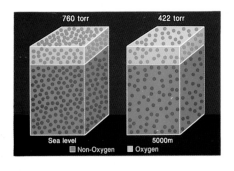

(opposite) Blouses of factory-made cloth have become extremely popular with nomad women.

(below) Custom dictates that riders walk their horses downhill and horses carry their riders uphill.

THE NOMADS BECOME PART OF CHINA: THE 1959 UPRISING

THE YEARS FOLLOWING THE 1951 signing of the 17 Point Agreement between Tibet and China did not alter the traditional social and economic system in Tibet. Lords such as the Panchen Lama oversaw their fiefs, while the Tibetan government headed by the Dalai Lama continued to administer Tibet. The Pala nomads remained just as they had before the 1951 Agreement—the triennial livestock census was conducted in 1953 and 1956, and another was scheduled for the summer of 1959.

At the same time, however, Chinese troops and officials entered Tibet and began building political and logistical infrastructure. As the years passed, resentment and hostility between Tibetans and Chinese increased, and after 1956, a guerrilla movement opposed to the Chinese began to operate in Tibet. The long-term viability of the 17 Point Agreement's balance between Tibetan autonomy and Chinese sovereignty came increasingly into question. Matters came to a head on March 10, 1959 when Tibetans in Lhasa rose up against the Chinese while the Dalai Lama and a large segment of his government fled to exile in India. The Chinese crushed the uprising and set about to destroy the various guerilla bands.

One of these, led by the nomad Bo Argon, was operating out of Nakdzang, a nomad area immediately north-northwest of Pala. One of the Pala nomads explained what happened:

> He (Bo Argon) sent messengers (in 1959) to us and all the surrounding nomad groups telling us to join him in opposing the Chinese. We, however, decided to follow the lead of our lord, the Panchen Lama... (Q. Why did you do this?) We had never seen a Chinese and had no idea what the situation was in China or even Lhasa. So when our lord and his officials said it would be best not to join the uprising, our local leaders agreed. We followed their advice. This decision, however, quickly embroiled us in fighting with Bo Argon's forces which supported the Dalai Lama. They were angry at our decision and started raiding our encampments. In the ensuing clashes a number of our people were killed, and ultimately, in 1960, we had to call in the army (the People's Liberation Army) to protect ourselves against the rebels. They quickly defeated the rebels and brought peace to our area.

(pages 132–133) Sheep and goats spend fall, winter, and spring nights in corrals made from stone, sod, or mud bricks. The animals sleep outside in summer so that they do not get too "soft," as the nomads explain it.

Although the Panchen Lama was one of Tibet's greatest Buddhist incarnations, his decision against supporting the uprising reflects the internal history of 20th century Tibet. Paralleling the on-going external conflict between the Tibetan central government and China, within Tibet there was on-going conflict over the authority and prerogatives of the central government vis-a-vis the rights of the lords, particularly the religious and monastic lords. Nowhere was this more dramatic than the dispute between the 13th Dalai Lama and the 9th Panchen Lama, which ended in 1924 when the Panchen fled into exile in China rather than accept an increase in taxes levied by the Dalai Lama's government. Attempts were made to reconcile the differences over the next 13 years, but in 1937, the 9th Panchen Lama died in exile in an ethnic Tibetan region of Western China (Qinghai Province)—bitter but unbowed. His successor, the 10th Panchen Lama, was found by his entourage in this same area. Living in China and dependent upon Chinese support and good will, the Panchen Lama's staff sent congratulatory telegrams to Mao Zedung after the communists emerged victorious from the civil war, and from the start strongly allied themselves with the communists. The 10th Panchen Lama first set foot in Tibet only in April 1952, accompanied by units of the People's Liberation Army.

Thus, when political events unravelled in Tibet in 1959, the Panchen Lama decided that the best course of action was to work with the Chinese and instructed his subjects and followers not to oppose the government, and the Pala nomads acquiesced, believing that if they did so they would be able to continue their traditional way of life. They were, of course, dead wrong. Unbeknownst to them, the 1959 uprising would precipitate a series of changes that would almost totally destroy the way of life that they and their ancestors had followed for centuries. But this did not happen all at once.

The Chinese employed harsh measures to suppress the 1959 revolt but afterward, partially at the urging of the Panchen Lama, decided that the Tibetan masses were not ready for radical communist economic reforms like those already in place in China proper. They concluded that rather than forcibly impose agricultural and nomadic communes, Tibet would be brought only *gradually* into the "socialist line." Accordingly, the Tibetan economy was not collectivized immediately, and the household was left as the basic unit of economic production in both the agricultural and nomadic areas.

In *Lagyab lhojang,* the triennial livestock census planned for 1959 was not carried out, and for the rest of the year the nomads simply continued using the pastures they had been allocated in 1956. By early 1960, however, a new administrative structure was organized on the district level, and changes began to be implemented.

Nomad males enjoy riding and racing horses at the annual summer fairs.

All Pala households were classified into a formal "class" structure, although it was not possible to identify a Marxist "exploiting" class since there were no absentee landlords—all rich nomads lived in Pala with their animals in the traditional society. Nomad households classified as "wealthy," or "representatives of the lord" *(ngatsab)*, were not expropriated, with the exception of one former leader who had actively supported the Dalai Lama's revolt. Throughout Tibet, aristocratic and monastic lords lost their estates, but those who were not involved in the uprising, including the Panchen Lama, were reimbursed by the government and allowed to keep their homes and personal property.

District officials organized a large meeting in Pala to announce these changes and organize a new local government, and new officials from the poor class were appointed. Debts were either rescinded or recalculated with reduced interest, and the livestock of the one expropriated family were divided among 20 poor nomad families. Culturally, organized religion was terminated—monasteries in *Lagyab lhojang* were closed and monks sent home. But on a day-to-day basis, nomads were permitted to maintain altars in their tents and perform private rites and prayers, and no attempt was made to constrain or eliminate nomad customs and taboos. Moreover, each nomad family continued to decide when to move its animals, and when to barter or sell its products.

In early 1961, production in Pala was revised by the implementation of a program known as "mutual aid" *(rogre)*. This program sought to inculcate a spirit of cooperation among the poor as a modest first step toward communal production. In Pala, the "middle" and "poor" classes were organized into "mutual-aid" groups consisting of several households sharing access to pastures. They were expected to cooperate in tasks such as herding, although all economic decisions remained rooted at the household level, as did all yields and income. Each household still owned its own livestock and sold or traded independently of the others in the "mutual-aid" group.

Creation of mutual-aid groups brought the first focused persecution of the former nomad "wealthy" class. Having already lost their authority and status, they were now isolated from the "masses" and not permitted to join the mutual-aid system. They also received poorer pastures and were forced to pay much higher taxes. Nevertheless, none of their animals were confiscated and they were permitted to continue hiring other poor nomads as servants and shepherds, albeit at higher wages than paid by the "middle" and "poor" classes. They also could still sell their products as they wished. Despite what in retrospect was handwriting on the wall, none of the wealthy-class nomad households had any inkling of what the future held for them.

The years 1960–66, therefore, passed in Pala with only minimal disruption of the nomads' way of life. There were no Chinese (Han) officials in the area and all contact was with Tibetans in the Tibetan language. Political-education meetings were held to inculcate the new communist ideology, but these were infrequent. Organized religion ended, but the private practice of religion continued. And crucially, the family persevered as the basic unit of production and consumption.

An elderly blind man spins wool in his threadbare tent. The old woman is a widow who lived alone until a few months prior when her tent pole split during a winter snowstorm, forcing her to move in with a neighbor and his wife.

THE CULTURAL REVOLUTION AND PASTORAL COMMUNES, 1966–81

THE EMERGENCE OF THE "GREAT PROLETARIAN CULTURAL REVOLUTION" in eastern China in late 1966 set in motion forces that engulfed the nomads in a decade of pain and suffering and almost destroyed their way of life. The Cultural Revolution and the Red Guards reached Lhasa almost immediately, immersing the more accessible regions of Tibet in a reign of terror and chaos. In more remote areas like Pala, the full force of the Cultural Revolution only arrived in 1968-70. Political "struggle sessions" and class conflict began in earnest, private religion was banned, and word reached the nomads that private ownership of livestock was to be replaced by people's communes.

Coming on top of their loss of religious freedom, the news that they would lose their livestock and freedom to work and trade as they saw fit was more than they could bear. They (and the nomads in the areas around them) rebelled. The overwhelming majority of Pala nomads adopted the name of one of Tibet's two Red Guard groups (*Gyenlo* or "revolutionaries"), and interpreted the intent of Mao's call to "pull down those in authority" to mean expelling the local government officials and reinstituting *complete religious and economic freedom* under their own leadership. Since the army in China had declared itself neutral in the struggle between the competing Red Guard groups, the nomads mistakenly believed it would also remain neutral in their struggle for religious and economic freedom. The Pala rebels arrested the few Pala nomads who supported the pro-communist-party Red Guard group (*Nyamdre* or "alliance"), captured and executed two district-level Tibetan officials who had been especially cruel in implementing "class struggle," and drove out the rest, taking control of their area for three months during the summer of 1969.

Their success was short-lived. Guided by loyal Tibetan cadre, the People's Liberation Army, as in 1959, once again came to Pala —but this time to attack rather than support the nomads. Armed almost solely with matchlock rifles and swords, the nomads' rebellion disintegrated immediately. The rebel leaders were arrested and punished and a commune system was instituted in Pala.

(pages 138–139) Nomad custom is to dismount and lead one's horse into camp.

At this time, the class background of each nomad family was reexamined, and households were reclassified as "poor," "middle," or "rich" based on factors such as the number of servants and hired hands they had. The "rich" were designated as "exploiters" of the masses and "class enemies," and overnight, their lives were turned topsy turvy.

Wanam recalled for us the day in 1970 when the local Tibetan leaders of the Cultural Revolution suddenly appeared before his tent and, without any prior warning, ordered him out and expropriated all his wealth.

> They called me a reactionary and a class enemy and told me that from today on all my animals and goods were confiscated and I must live under the "guidance" of the people just as the poorest of the poor lived in the old society. We had about 1,200 sheep and goats and 100 yak at this time. Right then and there they ripped off my earring, rings, necklace, and took my silver flint-striker and bullet holder. They also confiscated my new sheepskin robe saying that it was too good for the likes of a class enemy like me. In its place they gave me an old, worn one. But this was not all. They also took all of my family's household possessions and food stores, leaving us only one pot, one bag of 55 pounds of barley grain per person, and a little tsamba. And then they took away our fine yak-hair tent giving us in its place an old, tattered canvas tent. We were stunned—our whole life's wealth was eliminated in a matter of minutes. We didn't know how we would survive since they also said that we could not join the people's commune but had to fend for ourselves, alone and without help. Our sole means of support were the 40 goats they left us (eight goats per person), only 10 of which were milk goats.

Another former class enemy told us:

> They forced me to stand before "the people" bent over at the waist, eyes looking at the ground, for hours while individuals yelled and screamed at me for exploiting them. Yanchen (a female official) even jumped and sat on my back like I was a horse while berating me for my crimes. But I never understood any of this. I hadn't mistreated anyone. I was rich and had lots of animals, but that was due to my own capabilities, so how could that be a crime. It was very difficult. At first I didn't want to admit my crimes but it was futile and I soon decided my only hope for survival was to play along and admit to everything while demonstrating my change of heart. Two years after the commune began they allowed me join it. Before that I could barely survive on the few goats they left with me. I hunted a lot but with no gun I had to climb above the cornered animals and kill them by throwing down rocks. Occasionally, I got some private work from commune members such as tanning skins, but we were always on the verge of starvation. After we were in the commune life was still hard but at least the fear of starvation was not ever-present.

Some nomads scrambled to change or avoid a "bad-class" label by denouncing spouses or parents. Trinley, for example, was a poor man who had married the only daughter of a wealthy nomad and became a part of her household. Since he was not in the "wealthy" class by birth, he and his son caved in to the suggestions of officials that they now show their true class origins by divorcing (and denouncing) the wife/mother. Trinley did so and was made a commune leader as a reward. His former wife ultimately died alone from what appears to be a combination of disease, malnutrition, and despair. Trinley nowadays is so ridden with guilt that he is only partially functional.

Nomad communes were relatively simple to implement despite the seeming incongruity of the concepts of "commune" and "nomads." The subsistence technology (milking, churning, herding, moving, and so forth) remained identical, but the nomads were transformed from private owners of animals to holders of a share in the commune's property—or as one nomad more bluntly put it, "We were nothing more than servants of the commune. The commune took all our animals and productive implements such as pails and churns, and we had to do whatever work they told us."

The old pattern of winter trading trips to obtain grain continued, but now transactions were between nomad communes and farming communes rather than economically independent families.

When we asked the nomads whether the commune paid them for their animals and equipment, one man explained, "The 'class enemies' of course got nothing. For the rest of us, after taking all the animals and wealth, they assigned monetary values to each item in order to calculate the total worth of the commune. This figure, divided by the number of 'members,' established the monetary value of a single person's share. If the animals and equipment you 'gave' were worth more than this amount, you got some money back. I was classified as a "middle-class" nomad because I had had 200 sheep and 20 yak, and I actually got back 500 *yuan* at this time. But I lost all my freedom."

Unlike the traditional period when each family performed all the necessary productive activities, during the commune era individuals often specialized in only one or two activities such as herding yak or milking. All the pastoral tasks such as milking, shearing wool, and so forth were assigned a work-point value from one to 10, for example, milking received 10 points whereas spinning wool thread only three and yak herding five. Work "points" were awarded each day depending on the nature and amount of each person's work. and once each month, the commune secretary rode to each encampment to record in a master ledger the daily activities (and points) of each nomad over the previous 30 days. Each nomad was given a small booklet in which he or she could record daily work; illiterates without friends to help had to memorize their work record until the secretary arrived.

The new government policy permits the open practice of religion. This elderly woman faces the local mountain god and does her daily prostration prayers. Her prayer wheel is carefully set on a cloth beside her.

Each year, the commune's total production less its taxes to the government was converted to a monetary figure and divided by the total number of work points accrued during the year. This yielded a cash value for each work point. Each nomad then obtained an equal, but minimal amount of food and other products. This was usually just a bare subsistence level. The value of this amount was then subtracted from the household's total work points. If a household had leftover work points after this, it received additional goods and/or cash, but if it were short work points, it had to repay the commune or go into debt to it.

Some households with many able workers did reasonably well under the commune's system of payment, but the quality of life for the overwhelming majority of nomads deteriorated markedly in comparison with the previous decade and the traditional society. This was partially the result of the high taxes and forced quota sales and partly because the nomads did not care for the commune's livestock as carefully as their own. But it was also because officials interested in enhancing their own reputations falsely claimed increases in production. Paying the accompanying increase in the total taxes required a greater percentage of real production and left less to be divided.

Work was constant—seven days a week, with massive "public-works" projects such as fencing off pastures with stone walls undertaken when there was no real work. People had no control over their lives. They were powerless and felt like slaves, ordered here and there by their new masters. One nomad who had been poor in the old society poignantly expressed the general feeling, "At least before the commune if you were hungry you could always find work as a herder or servant, or outright beg for food, but during the commune, you just stayed hungry."

However, no attempt was made to diminish the geographic scope of pastoralism during the commune period either by expropriating nomad pastureland, resettling nomads in agricultural areas, or resettling Tibetan or Chinese (Han) farmers in nomad areas. Full-scale pastoralism, therefore, continued during the Cultural Revolution. On the other hand, the traditional culture came under severe attack.

The nomads' hatred of this system derives not just from the economic hardships they endured. As much or more they hated the class struggle sessions and the complete destruction of all remnants of Buddhism in their society. The policy known as "destroying the four olds" (old ideas, old culture, old customs and old habits) was energetically implemented with the aim of eliminating the traditional culture and creating in its place a new homogeneous and atheistic communist culture. Private religious activities were forbidden, religious buildings including monasteries and prayer walls were torn down, and the nomads were forced to abandon the deeply held values and customs that were the essence of their cultural identity. For example, men were required to cut their distinctive hair-style of bangs and two braids, and women were required to break the strong taboo against females slaughtering animals. This was a terrible period since the nomads' values, norms and morals were deliberately turned upside down and, furthermore, food was often inadequate. The propaganda and class struggle sessions conducted by Tibetan cadre contradicted and ridiculed everything the nomads understood and felt, creating feelings of anxiety, guilt, worthlessness, and low self-esteem. In a sense, the government attempted to reduce Tibetan ethnic identity to language alone; all the rest of their rich culture—their values and customs—was rejected as super-stition, deceit, and exploitation. Chinese policy during this period sought to maintain pastoral production but destroy the social and cultural fabric of the nomads' traditional way of life. From the nomads' point of view, they had become an exploited subject class treated far worse than they had been under the "serfdom" of the old society. None of them believed they would ever again see a day when they would be allowed to follow their traditional way of life again—the "old society" appeared dead!

taking horses out to graze

CHINA'S POST-CULTURAL REVOLUTION TIBET POLICY

HISTORY IS NOT STRAIGHTFORWARD AND YESTERDAY'S inconceivable often becomes today's commonplace. The end of the Cultural Revolution in China proper in 1976 and the destruction of the "Gang of Four" brought a new group of leaders to the fore in the Chinese Communist Party whose views changed the fate of the Pala nomads. Holding an entirely different economic and cultural philosophy from Mao and the Gang of Four, they viewed the "Cultural Revolution" as a catastrophe for China and terminated communes, implementing a more market-oriented rural economic system called the "responsibility" system. Responsibility for production was shifted from the commune to the household.

The full impact of these changes reached Pala in 1981 when the hated commune system was ended. Overnight, all the commune's animals were divided equally among its members. Every nomad —infants one week old, teenagers, adults, the elderly—received the same share of 37 animals: five yak, 25 sheep, and seven goats. A household of five, therefore, obtained 25 yak, 125 sheep and 35 goats in addition to the 30–40 "private" goats it had been allowed to maintain during the commune era. Each household regained complete responsibility over its livestock, managing them according to their own plans and decisions. Pastureland was allocated at the same time to small groups of three to six households living in the same home-base encampment.

An added benefit was Beijing's decision to exclude Tibetan peasants and nomads from all taxes and quota sales until at least 1990 because of the poverty of the Tibet Autonomous Region. Without taxes and with careful management and hard work, the number of livestock each household received in 1981 fulfilled basic subsistence needs and should have yielded a modest surplus as well. Several nomads commented that it would have put them just within the "lower middle class" in the old society.

With the shift in Chinese politics, portraits of Mao Zedung are no longer fashionable. This nomad couldn't quite bring himself to burn the photo. Instead, he put it on a pile of dried dung stacked on top of his windbreak wall.

Monks from a local nomad monastery set up a "temple tent" at a summer fair at the district headquarters in 1986, performing prayers and giving blessings to a stream of nomad supplicants.

The new Chinese leadership also instituted policies eliminating persecution on the basis of class background, and attempted to right some of the terrible injustices that took place during the Cultural Revolution by monetary restitutions to the "class enemies" whose animals and belongings had been confiscated. A number of Pala nomads received restitutions, and one who was among the richest in the old society received thousands of Chinese dollars *(yuan)*—a small fortune in Tibet where, by comparison, the annual salary of a university instructor in Lhasa is about 2,500-3,000 *yuan*.

The new policies also brought a new local government to *Lagyab lhojang*. Pala, which had been a commune, became a *shang (xiang)*. The *shang* has little real power and functions primarily as a liaison between the government and the nomads, transmitting, for example, higher level decisions and orders to the individual nomad households, and collecting information on topics such as the number of sheep and goats and passing it up to the district. It controls no income or resources and has little to no impact on locally relevant policy. It does, however, play an important role in the arena of family law and local disputes, hearing and deciding cases usually in consultation with the local communist-party secretary and the district officials at Tsatsey. Because of this, the nomads are concerned about the quality of their local leaders.

The two *shang* heads are elected from a slate of candidates chosen by the district officials. Despite the external control of nominations, we found that the list of candidates in Pala in recent elections included most nomads we would have thought appropriate. In fact, one of the two *shang* heads during our stay was a former monk and class enemy who is highly respected and liked by virtually all nomads. As our research ended, a new government was about to be installed which was supposed to place even nominations for local officials in the hands of the nomads. The plan called for a nominating election to precede the official election.

One of the most notable aspects of the post-1980 reforms was the reinstatement of considerable religious freedom. During the period of our fieldwork in Pala the nomads were free to practice their religion as they chose, and religion had regained its importance in their lives. Nomads were pursuing the cycle of religious rites that typified the traditional society. Most families had small altars in their tents and flew prayer flags from their tent poles and guylines. Nomads no longer feared open displays of religion; some even wore Dalai Lama buttons and others displayed his photograph openly in their tents. Individuals turning prayer wheels, counting rosaries and doing prostrations were common sights, and even one of Pala's four communist-party members now intones Buddhist prayers. Even government functions, such as the summer horse-race fairs at the district, included unofficial, but open, religious components—for example, monks reading prayers in a special large "temple" tent.

As nomads grow older they turn toward religion. Here a nomad sits in the sun beside his tent reading his daily prayers from a traditional prayer book. The prayers are printed by hand carved wood blocks on the long strips of paper on his lap.

The depth of these changes was pointedly illustrated one afternoon in December 1987 when a few nomads brought a newly purchased radio to our tent and and sat listening to the Government of India's (All India Radio's) Tibetan-language shortwave broadcast of news, Tibetan music and religious prayers. Because they had the volume turned up and our tent was just a few feet from that of a party leader, we asked if they weren't concerned that he would overhear. The nomads laughed at this suggestion and jokingly retorted, "Why should he care? He listens also."

Nomads make pilgrimages to monasteries and holy sites and travel to visit Lamas without asking anyone's permission. Some are also actively supporting the reemergence of monasticism by donating animals and food to help rebuild small local monasteries, and by hiring monks to conduct prayers at life crises, e.g., the death of a household member. The small Drigung Kajupa monastery in Tsatsey, rubble when we first arrived in 1986, was rebuilt with local funds and functional when we departed in 1988. The comments of one old woman epitomize the depth of the feelings involved: "I feel sorry for all those who died during the commune period because they couldn't do religious prayers and have the proper death rites. It was a terrible time for us. But I feel happy to be again able to recite my prayers every day and do prostrations and circumambulations (around the prayer wall)."

The old woman sits against a sod brick wall counting prayers on her rosary and watching life in the camp go on.

(left) Young and old monks at their evening prayer session inside a small monastery rebuilt a few years earlier.

(below) Villagers come to nomad country every summer to work tanning skins, building prayer walls and storehouses, carving religious prayer stones, and forming clay statues. A prosperous nomad commissioned the molded clay tablet statues that are drying in the sun beside a villagers' traveling tent, paying an adult goat for them.

These traditional practices did not reappear all at once or in an orderly sequence. At first, the nomads feared that the new policy was a devious trick launched to expose pockets of "rightist" thinking, and individuals were reluctant to take the lead and risk being singled out. Change occurred gradually as individuals took single actions that, in effect, tested the general policy. When no protest or punishment came from the Tsatsey district officials above them (all of whom are ethnic Tibetans), the desirable practice spread, and this process is still going on.

The reemergence of nomad "mediums" (individuals whom deities possess and speak through) exemplifies this. It is an aspect of the traditional Tibetan Buddhist religious system that is considered unnecessary "superstition" not only by the communists but to an extent also by the refugee government-in-exile. Yet it reappeared in Pala in the winter of 1987 when an adult in one camp took ill and was in great pain for days before he died. A man from the same encampment went into trance spontaneously during the illness and was possessed by a deity who gave a prognosis and explanation of the disease. When no official criticism of this event occurred in the ensuing weeks and months, he and others fashioned the traditional costume worn by mediums, and he is now sought by others in Pala in cases of illness.

During the Cultural Revolution, monasteries were torn down and prayer stones carried away for other uses. Local monks rebuilding their monastery have rounded up many of the monastery's old carved prayer stones.

What has been occurring, therefore, is a form of what anthropologist Anthony Wallace calls cultural revitalization.[8] In their contact with the dominant and alien Marxist cultural system, the nomads were told that their traditional leaders were contemptible enemies of the people and their old values and norms were immoral and exploitive. Compelled to abandon the traditional beliefs and symbols that gave meaning to the world around them and to actively embrace a new "communist" culture consisting of norms and values that they considered repugnant, they experienced a crisis of morality and meaning. This was further exacerbated when they had to put the new morality into practice by persecuting and physically punishing the newly defined "class enemies," many of whom were friends, spouses, and kinsmen. China's new post-1980 policies created conditions wherein individual Tibetans were able to resurrect a more satisfying culture by readopting traditional components of their cognitive and affective systems and discarding components of the "revolutionary" culture they had been forced to profess. They have done this not just with religion, but with all facets of their way of life. For example, as we have seen, hunting wild animals and butchering livestock are again taking on the stigma they had in the traditional society.

An incident that occurred during our fieldwork in Pala illustrates the extent to which the traditional beliefs have reemerged. A former "poor-class" nomad who had been a local official during the commune period sold a lactating sheep to a trader before milking it, therein breaking a traditional nomad taboo. Nomads believe that this could negatively affect the milk production of the entire camp, and another man in the same camp, a former persecuted "class enemy," became incensed. He berated the seller and words soon escalated to pushing and fighting. Both separately took the case before the local government, the "poor-class" nomad arguing that the former "wealthy-class" nomad was looking down on him because of his poor-class background and was trying to impose reactionary superstitions on him. He was so angry at his neighbor that he actually moved to a different encampment in Pala. The local and district level officials, however, were not impressed with his anachronistic perspective and did not side with him as they would have before the current reforms. Instead they fined both men for fighting, validating, in the process, the ability of former class enemies to bring cases against those from the "poor class," as well as the legitimacy of traditional taboos for contemporary life.

On another occasion, a goat owned by one of Pala's four communist-party members was accidentally strangled by the rope that tied it during milking. It was already dusk so when the family head put the corpse in one of his empty corrals, we thought he was protecting it from predators for the night and would slaughter it the next day. We, in fact, were out of meat and hoped to be able to buy a few pounds from him. The next morning, however, we saw his brother-in-law carrying the carcass toward the lake. When we went to ask him about this, he explained that the carcass had been thrown away. Surprised at this waste of good meat, we inquired about the reason and learned that the nomads do not eat meat which had been killed by females—and that in this case they considered that the goat had been killed by the female milkers, albeit inadvertently.

(opposite) Throughout Tibet local people are rebuilding monasteries that were destroyed during the Cultural Revolution. In 1986 Tongling monastery was still in ruins, but by 1988 the monks had collected donations from the local nomads and hired Tibetan villagers to rebuild the main prayer-hall complex.

(below) With few roads in Western Tibet, in most places trucks simply follow the flat plains. Here a truck carrying some nomads to the hay-cutting area has bogged down in sand.

Current marriage patterns also reveal the reemergence of traditional attitudes and values. A number of today's wealthy families, for example, favorably consider a potential spouse's high-status family background from the old society, and almost all nomads now refuse to marry someone from the traditional "unclean" stratum. Similarly, nomad practitioners of traditional Tibetan medicine are again active in the area, and traditional singing and dancing often spontaneously erupt when the young from several camps come together.

And in the broader Tibetan social arena, the nomads have resumed the traditional practice of hiring scores of villagers who travel 20-30 days to Pala each summer to work tanning sheep and goat skins, carving prayer stones, molding clay figurines of deities, building prayer walls, and constructing storehouses and residences in exchange for live animals. This practice not only is reestablishing social boundaries between farmers and nomads, but is also reaffirming the social worth of the nomads' pastoral way of life and the view that theirs is the easier, more productive life.

The post-1980 cultural policy in Tibet, therefore, has allowed individual nomads in Pala to revitalize their cultural system, constructing a more satisfying and coherent view of the world around them and, in the process, reestablishing pride in their customs. Although all nomads realize that the government is the final arbiter of how far this process can go, and although there was considerable individual variation in the extent and timing of this process (some nomads being less interested in adhering to traditional religious and social values), the bulk of the traditional cultural system was essentially operational again in 1988, and the nomads were pleased by this thoroughly unexpected turn of events.

(opposite) Blindness does not prevent this elderly woman from conducting her daily prayers.

(below) The traditional nomad greeting for visitors is touching foreheads and asking "You haven't had any difficulties, have you?"

However, the nomads' knowledge (and fear) that the current government could intervene again at any time and impose its alien values has left a feeling of vulnerability, anxiety, and anger, despite their positive objective assessment of the current situation.

These fears about the stability of the current state ideology have been exacerbated by their feelings of powerlessness at the local level. At the very nadir of a vertical chain of command, they feel their views and concerns are not taken seriously, notwithstanding a system of sending delegates to a "People's Congress" at the county level. The nomads complain that new decrees and orders are passed down from above and, even when condradictory or ill thought out, are enforced.

District and county officials continue to exert tremendous control over the nomads' lives through their control of political, legal, and economic institutions. The nomads are reluctant to openly disagree with district and county officials, and especially to go over their heads by appealing to higher authorities to protest actions and policies. They feel that they have no leverage against officials who use their powerful positions for their own gain or to help friends and favorites, and fear, not without reason, that any officials whom they challenge and criticize will find an opportunity to pay them back with interest. The following discussion of controversies regarding illegal quota sales and forced livestock reductions illustrates well the nature of this powerlessness.

All of this has retarded development of positive attitudes toward the state, and to a considerable extent, underlies the obvious incongruity between the positive objective effects of Beijing's new policy in Tibet and the Tibetans' often negative reaction to the government that enacted them.

(left) The traditional nomad male hair style consists of bangs and two braids.

ECONOMIC AND SOCIAL CHANGE UNDER THE NEW POLICIES

THE RELAXATION OF RESTRICTIONS ON RELIGIOUS FREEDOM and free enterprise has had important ramifications for the nomads' standard of living and their internal social organization.

Trade for grain, tea, and other products has always been an integral component of the subsistence economy of nomad families. These individual trading activities were terminated during the Cultural Revolution but quickly reemerged under the new economic policy. At present, there are five types of trade in Pala: 1) trade with the government at the district and county levels; 2) private trade with farmers located 20- to 30-days' walk to the southeast along the fringe of the Changtang; 3) trade with farmers and traders who come to the Changtang in summer to exchange products and labor for livestock or livestock products; 4) trade with other nomads—for example, for horses and livestock and; 5) a newly emerging trade with Shigatse, the large Tibetan city two- to three-days' distant by truck (and two months by yak caravan). Categories 2, 3 and 4 were the traditional types of barter trade.

The new economic policy in the Tibet Autonomous Region gives nomads and farmers the right to sell all their products to whomever they want. Unlike the peasants in China proper, they do not have to pay taxes or make quota sales to the government until at least 1990. However, this thoughtful policy has been partially undermined and the nomads are being coerced to sell the bulk of their wool and cashmere to the government's trade office through a system of quota sales, although the officials represent these as voluntarily negotiated contracts. Private trade in the restricted items is permitted only after these quotas have been fulfilled.

The reason for this practice is money—wool and cashmere sales generate a tremendous amount of profit for the county and prefecture trade offices. The profit motive here is not individual but institutional—it is primarily aimed at generating profit for a governmental office in order to enhance the officials' reputations rather than lining their own pockets.

On the other hand, because these officials want to give the appearance that these "contracts" are entered into voluntarily, they cannot pay the nomads so little as to provoke a protest to Lhasa. Thus, the price of cashmere has increased from 125-200% over the past four years, and the price of wool 50% over the past three years. Real implementation of open markets for wool and cashmere would have yielded better prices for the nomads, but these increases have been substantial and have more than offset the increases in the price of grains and other imported staples such as tea.

Officials also work energetically to keep the district store well stocked, frequently trucking in grain and other products such as tea. Because they offer the nomads a reasonable, albeit slightly lower, price than that available on the open market, and because they offer either cash or goods as well as the convenience of having to travel only three days to the district headquarters (rather than a month to trade with more distant farmers), most nomads would probably deal with the government's trade office even if they had free choice. However, they do not have that option and greatly resent this illegal practice which they feel powerless to dislodge. This appears to be a case where thoughtful and sympathetic national-level policies for Tibet are being contravened at lower levels. Our discussion with nomads in adjacent counties indicate that this is not an isolated problem, and that the same practices are being employed in other nomad regions.

Notwithstanding the controversial quota sales, it is clear that the nomads' main livestock products are increasing in value under the new market-oriented economy. This, coupled with the tax concession, has improved the standard of living in Pala despite an overall eight percent decrease in herd size since commune dissolution in 1981. Nomads, for example, are buying traditional items such as pots, pans, clothes, jewelry and metal trunks, as well as new "luxury" items such as radios, tape cassettes, sewing machines, gasoline lamps and metal stoves and, as indicated above, hiring villagers to do a variety of manual labor tasks. Many have built new storehouses, and a few even new residences, costly investments since wood for the beams and pillars has to be brought from hundreds of miles away.

Traders come to the Changtang in summer to exchange grains and manufactured goods for wool, cashmere, pelts, and live animals.

The development of a crude road system on the Changtang has allowed trucks to reach almost all the nomad district headquarters. It has also allowed the wooden beams and pillars needed in house and storeroom construction to be imported cheaply from southeast Tibet. This nomad yak caravan hauls the precious wood the remaining three or four days to the nomad camps.

WOOL AND CASHMERE PROFITS

In 1987 the county trade office paid the nomads 3 *yuan* ($1=3.71 *yuan*) or 6.6 lbs. of grain per 1.1 lb. of wool and sold it to Shigatse prefecture for 3.9 *yuan*, generating a profit of 30%. They paid the nomads 13 *yuan* (or 29 lbs of grain) for 1.1 lbs. of cashmere, receiving 20 *yuan* from the prefecture for a 54% profit. Their profit on the total wool bought from the nomads was 131,305 *yuan* and on the cashmere was 67,927 *yuan*, making a gross profit 199,232 *yuan*. The gross profit is actually somewhat larger than this because most nomads take grain rather than money and the county obtains the grain for less than what it charges the nomads. From these gross profits the county has to pay the trade office workers' salaries, a 10% tax to the TAR government, and freight charges, but the profit clearly is still enormous given that the annual salary of a top official in the county is only about 2,500-3,000 *yuan*.

The high profitability of these livestock products continues as one moves up the market ladder. We calculate that the 160,485 lbs. of wool the Ngamring nomads had to sell to the government in 1987 brought the county a profit of about 131,305 *yuan* and the prefecture a profit of 379,327 *yuan*.

Shearing knives dull quickly, so whetstones are kept close at hand while shearing.

A Changtang road winds its way up a high pass.

The Pala nomads have begun to truck sheep for sale in Shigatse, a city three-days' ride to the southeast.

The alacrity with which the nomads have reverted back to the foundations of their traditional culture does not mean that important changes have not occurred, or that the nomads are completely resistant to change. Trade, for example, is one area where a process of transformation appears to have begun. Since wool traditionally was Tibet's main export item, the nomads have always been part of a larger market system. However, their dependence on distant Chinese and world markets has increased since commune dissolution. The construction of "truckable" roads from the county in Ngamring to the Tsatsey district in the mid-1970s has fostered this increasing entanglement. It signaled the beginning of a new era when the government (and eventually private traders) could easily bring grains and other commodities to the district headquarters, and thus to within three- to four-days' walk of virtually all Pala nomads. The subsequent completion (around 1980) of a feeder road from Tsatsey district to points in most *shang* (including Pala) made truck transport even more convenient, and has facilitated visits by Lhasa-based petty traders seeking cashmere, skins and (illegal) furs, as well as offering nomads the possibility of trading directly with new markets, such as the city of Shigatse which is just two- to three-days' distant by truck but close to a two-month trek by caravan.

So far, the nascent truck trade usually entails nomads renting space on one of the district's trucks to take livestock products (and even live sheep) to sell in Shigatse, the proceeds typically being used to purchase manufactured goods to resell to other nomads on the Changtang. A government loan policy has facilitated utilization and expansion of this option. In 1986, 1987, and 1988 loans were made available to nomads desiring to do business as part-time traders either in Shigatse or with other nomads farther west (where there is a thriving yak trade), and 17 households in Pala have received them, one for 10,000 *yuan* ($2,700 U.S.). The Shigatse trade has not yet proved to be highly profitable for most participants because of the high cost of renting truck space and the nomads' lack of business skills, but it is likely to increase in importance in the future as they gain familiarity with these new markets. Because it is voluntary, there is no resentment at this development which is perceived by the nomads as an opportunity.

All of this is gradually changing the pattern of Pala trade. Last year, for example, only three Pala households took the traditional one- to two-month winter trading trip with their carrying animals to adjacent farm areas. The rest conducted all their business with the district trade office and store at Tsatsey, or conducted most of it there and the remainder either with traders who came to the Changtang or, in a few cases, with traders in Shigatse. And although those who took the traditional winter trip bartered their (excess) products for prices higher than those paid by the Tsatsey trade office, this incremental profit is unlikely to motivate more nomads to make the long and arduous winter trip, given the harm it does to livestock and the fact that not much is actually left to sell after the forced sales to the district. Thus, it appears certain that the nomads will at least continue, and probably increase, their entanglement in distant market systems. Although this will likely produce future changes in the nomads' way of life, at present there is no reason to assume that it will be anything but profitable to the overall nomad economy.

Another striking consequence of China's post-1981 reform policy is the rapidity and extent to which economic and social differentiation has reemerged in Pala. Although all Pala's nomads in the old society were subjects of the Panchen Lama, tremendous class differences existed among the subjects. Rich families had huge herds and lived in relative luxury alongside a substantial stratum of herdless laborers, poor nomads, servants and beggars. Implementation of the commune in 1970 removed these disparities since all private ownership of the means of production ended at this time. During the decade of communal production, some economic differentiation resurfaced because households with more workers amassed more "work points," and commune officials consistently received the most "work points," but these differences were moderate, most nomads being equally poor. The dissolution of the commune in 1981 maintained a rough equality since all nomads in Pala received an equal number of livestock. However, in the ensuing seven years, some herds have increased while others have declined dramatically. Once again there are both very wealthy and very poor nomads. One household actually has no livestock at all.

While no households had less than 37 animals per person in 1981, 38% had less than 30 in 1988. At the high end of the continuum, the proportion of Pala households with more than 50 animals per person increased from 12% in 1981 to 25% in 1988. Ten percent of the households had more than 90 animals per person versus none in 1981. As a result of this process of economic differentiation, the richer 16% of the population in 1988 owned 33% of the animals while the poorer 33% of the population owned only 17% of the Pala animals.The past seven years of the family-based "responsibility" system has resulted in an increasing concentration of animals in the hands of a minority of newly wealthy households, and the emergence once again of a stratum of poor households with no or few animals.

The Changtang's bitter climate makes pastoralism the only economically viable mode of subsistence.

Whole-milk yogurt is plentiful and enjoyed daily in summer when all the livestock are giving milk.

(above) Nomad children play with whatever is available, including goat kids.

(below) The bright sun belies the bitter cold of a winter morning. This woman had to break the ice over the spring to get water.

These new poor subsist by working for rich nomads, several of whom now, as in the old society, regularly employ herders, milkers, and servants for long stretches of time. The memory of charges of exploitation leveled against employers has ensured that employees receive a decent wage—usually one sheep per month (equal to roughly 25 *yuan*) plus good food, and even clothes if the contract is for an entire year. Piecework is available too in the form of tailoring, spinning, weaving, wool shearing, cashmere combing, livestock slaughtering, grass cutting, and ear-mark cutting.

Ironically, the new economic policy in Pala has particularly benefited the former wealthy class, i.e., those who were expropriated and severely discriminated against during the Cultural Revolution. Four of the six households who now have 70 or more head of livestock per capita are former "wealthy class," and *all* of the former wealthy-class households are among those with the largest herds and most secure income.

This development is resented by a tiny minority of nomads who were powerful officials during the commune period and are unpopular and powerless today. Bitter at the loss of their authority and prestige, one once came to our tent and whispered, "You have to tell Lhasa about what is going on here." When we asked him what he meant he repeated himself. After much prodding, he finally said, "You know, the 'class enemies,' they are rising up again." The persistence of even a few people with such views creates an undercurrent of anxiety among most nomads who fear that the leftist pendulum will suddenly swing back and destroy all the new gains.

Examples of the household economies of poor and rich households in 1987-88 illustrate their very different strategies for survival.

Household #1 is wealthy and does not have to do any trading other than its forced quota sales to the district trade office. It was wealthy in the "old society" and was expropriated at the time the commune was created. It contains seven members: three adult males, two adult females, an elderly female, and a youth. In the summer of 1988 it owned 646 animals (278 sheep, 322 goat, 41 yak, and 5 horses) or 92 animals per person. The market value of these animals was about 31,000 *yuan* (or US$8,329). This household slaughtered 70 goats and sheep for meat (for itself and its hired hands). From its quota sales of wool, cashmere, *kulu*, sheep, and butter to the district, household #1 received 1,954 pounds of barley (297 pounds per person), roughly 550 pounds *more* than it needed for its basic subsistence. In addition to this, it obtained 294 *yuan* in cash which it used for other incidental expenses such as cooking oil, cigarettes, and radio batteries.

This household paid nine sheep/goats as wages to Tibetan farmers who tanned 90 sheep and goat skins, and another 32 sheep as wages to nomad herders and milkers. It owns two storehouses at its home-base encampment, and is gradually acquiring traditional and new luxury goods such as a cassette tape/radio player and several metal trunks. It is one of the wealthiest households in Pala.

By contrast, the head of household #2 was from a beggar household in the old society and is again one of the poorest in Pala. His household contains four persons (two adults and two young children) and requires about 550 pounds of grain for a year. In the summer of 1988 it owned only 64 livestock (seven yak, 29 sheep, and 28 goats) and had slaughtered just eight goats for meat in the fall of 1987. This household has just 16 animals per capita.

As its quota sales to the district, household #2 received just 86 pounds (43 pounds per person) of barley plus 73.5 *yuan* in cash. The household also bartered a sheep with a farmer-trader for about 83 pounds of *tsamba*, but still was roughly 220 pounds short of its subsistence (barley) needs. The male head of the household, therefore, was forced to engage in a variety of tasks for wages that took him away from home for over four months of the year:

1. He worked two months as a herder for household #1. He ate his own food for one month in order to earn three sheep as salary instead of the normal two.

2. He spun 30 pounds of yak hair for two households and received two goats as wages.

3. He worked two months as herder for a household in another encampment and received two sheep as salary.

4. He snared one antelope, ate the meat, and sold the skin for 50 *yuan* to a passing Lhasa-based trader.

5. He butchered over 100 sheep/goats and seven yak for other nomad households, receiving payment of about 88 pounds of grain, plus miscellaneous entrails.

The grain, money, and free meals deriving from his labor provided enough supplementary income to meet his household's grain needs. But the household also required other products such as tea, cooking oil, clothes, matches, cigarettes (both husband and wife eventually decided to give up smoking to save money), tobacco, etc. Normally it would have acquired these by selling the sheep and goats the household head earned as wages, but in 1987 it received 275 pounds of barley as welfare from the district and therefore was able to add these animals to its herd, increasing its potential for future income.

These two examples reveal the tremendous differences that have developed in the seven years since dissolution of the commune. The poor household now must work for wages, accept "welfare" from the government, and subsist with little meat and the poorest-quality diet. The rich household, on the other hand, now, as rich households did in the old society, hires poor nomads to do many of the difficult tasks and consumes a high-quality and more varied diet. It is not possible to account here in detail for these differences, but in general they derive from a concatenation of factors such as luck, skill, consumption philosophy and diligence. The nomads see this dramatic change as a part of the natural (traditional) way of things, and themselves accept these outcomes since all households had (and have) equal opportunity to succeed or fail as their luck and skill allows. And although they all agree that economic polarization is not as advanced as it was in the old society, it seems likely to us (and the nomads) that the newly "poor" households such as the one just described will form a permanent laborer stratum.

Despite the forced quota sales and the economic differentiation, all nomads reported that economic life is much better these days than during the commune period when people often went hungry. The main reason for this, as indicated earlier, is the absence of taxes and the increase in the value of nomad products, particularly cashmere. Also important is the great demand for laborers in Pala and the relatively high wages being paid. It is also noteworthy that welfare is preventing complete destitution for a number of families. In 1987, for example, 10 households (18%) received welfare from the county amounting to 2,000 pounds of barley.

But while there clearly has been a substantial improvement in the overall standard of living in Pala since 1981, by objective measures most of these nomads are still very poor. Their tents rarely have rugs and they often wear tattered clothes. Many can afford to eat meat for just four to five months a year and a number do not even have a yak-hair tent, living instead in small patched cloth tents that are frequently torn and battered by the fierce winds. Economically, they still have a long way to go to approach the standard of living of most Han villagers in eastern China.

CONSERVATION OF THE ENVIRONMENT AND THE FUTURE OF TIBET'S INDIGENOUS NOMADIC PASTORALISTS

PRESERVATION OF CHINA'S GRASSLAND ENVIRONMENTS is an issue of concern among scientists and development planners in China today. The extent of ecological degradation is unclear, but the English-language *China Daily* newspaper (discussing an article in China's *Economic Daily*) reported that 15% of China's grasslands had deteriorated by the mid '70s, and that this had increased to 30% by the mid-'80s (*China Daily* 1987).

The existence of a grassland ecological crisis in China proper has been extended to the more remote and underpopulated region of Tibet, where the government has intervened to protect the environment. However, the evidence of overgrazing in Tibet appears to be based not on the direct monitoring of the environment, but rather on inferences and assumptions derived from livestock census data—for example, on data such as that produced by a major Chinese study on pastoralism in Tibet which reported that there was a 113% increase in the number of livestock in Tibet in the 23-year period from 1958-1981 despite the disruption of the 1959 uprising and the Cultural Revolution. The government's attitude appears also to be strongly influenced by the view widely held in the field of economic development that *traditional* pasture strategies are inefficient and destructive and pose an obstacle to implementation of efficient livestock production and range management. The government of the TAR, therefore, is following the policy prevalent throughout the rest of China and intervening to reduce herd size — placing limits on the number of livestock individuals can own or ordering annual or occasional herd reductions such as a 20% reduction implemented in Pala in 1987. It also is working to develop programs that will replace the traditional system with modern methods of animal husbandry, including the introduction of new species of livestock and vegetation.

In Pala this has produced a classic confrontation between the government and the indigenous pastoralists.

*Children as young as 7 and 8 years of age
are effective herders.*

The Pala nomads disagree with the government's view as well as the specific proposition that there is overgrazing in Pala. They contend that their traditional system has allowed them to subsist on the Changtang for uncounted centuries precisely because it and their livestock are well adapted to the plateau's extremely harsh conditions and do not destroy the viability of the pasturelands. The nomads' pastoral management strategy reasons that insurance against the inevitable bad years of drought, snow, or disease lies in increasing their herd size during good years. Each household, therefore, believes that prosperity requires having many livestock which are culled only for food or trade, i.e., never just to maintain an artificially determined herd size or internal composition. They claim that this strategy does not result in rapid growth of livestock numbers.

The nomads' emphasis on increasing herd sizes, however, is precisely what appears ecologically destructive to most officials, and it is not surprising that it has received little sympathy in China and the TAR. As one Tibetan county official commented about Pala and the surrounding nomad areas: "The nomads have to be educated to understand that just rearing more and more animals is not the answer." This attitude, which appears pervasive among government officials, dismisses the traditional local system as destructive, and rejects *a priori* the possibility that it might allow the nomads a decent livelihood over the long term without exponential growth in herds and the destruction of their resource base. Our findings, in fact, suggest that the traditional pastoral system was sophisticated and may have done just what the nomads claim.

The 1987 decree ordering the Pala nomads to reduce their livestock by 20% reflected the government's concern that overgrazing exists. The need to balance herd size with available pasture obviously is fundamental to ecological-conservation theory and practice, but overgrazing is a *possibility* whose presence or absence must be ascertained through detailed analyses of the animal-pasture relationship in any given area—it cannot simply be assumed to exist either by casual observation or data from other areas.

One of the crucial questions, therefore, is whether the Pala herds are actually growing rapidly. We collected livestock census data from the post-commune period. These data reveal an overall eight percent decrease —a four-percent decrease in the number of livestock in Pala between commune dissolution in 1981 and 1987, and another four-percent decrease after the 20% reduction decree between (1987 and 1988). The nomads' strategy of herd maximization, therefore, clearly did not result in increasing numbers of livestock in Pala over this period. Given this, it is reasonable to ask why the officials had such concerns.

a nomad camp

We suspect that county and district officials had an incorrect impression that herd size had increased. Specifically, we surmise that they inadvertently under-enumerated the number of livestock extant in 1981, the critical baseline year of commune dissolution, and thus overestimated the increase from then to 1987. We discovered that at the time of commune dissolution only the animals owned by the commune were divided equally. An additional number of animals comprising the "private holdings" (*gersha*) of the nomads remained the property of each household *and do not appear in the 1981 records*. In Pala, these "private animals" totaled about 1,800 goats—that is to say, the official total was roughly 20% lower than the actual number. When these 1,800 private animals are not taken into account, the records indicate an increase in herd size of 15% from 1981 to 1987, or a 2.4% annual growth rate rather than the actual four-percent decline. It is not unlikely that officials in this county (and possibly other nomads areas of the TAR) were unaware of this discrepancy when they ordered the forced reduction of herds. In the face of these flawed data, it is easy to understand the dismay of the Pala nomads at this order which doubled the existing four-percent decrease in herd size.

Additional data also suggest that the balance of livestock, people, and pasture in Pala is not degrading or overgrazing the pastureland.

Lambs and kids keep each other warm through winter nights in small covered pens.

First, there are an abundance and diversity of wild ungulates such as antelope, wild asses, gazelles, and blue sheep. We always encountered herds of the first three when traveling between camps. This situation is generally not found in areas where severe overgrazing has degraded rangeland.

Second, the nomads reported and we confirmed that in 1986 some of their more distant fall grazing areas were not used at all since the households that held rights over them decided their nearer pastures were adequate.

Third, on several occasions the members of an encampment willingly accepted a household from another camp even though it substantially increased the number of livestock using that camp's grazing areas. In one instance, for example, the new household's livestock represented an increase of 44% in the total number of animals held by the receiving camp. When queried about this, the nomads indicated that they still had considerable leeway with regard to stocking.

Fourth, qualitative indications of overgrazing were absent. Plant communities remain rich in species; we collected over 75 species of herbaceous plants from actively grazed rangeland, and speculate that there are more to be catalogued in other grazing areas. The observation that in most Pala pastures nearly every perennial grass plant was able to attain seed-bearing stage in 1987 suggests that degradation of the vegetational component of the ecosystem is probably not occurring. Furthermore, we found no visual evidence of severe erosion or soil compaction. Although Pala has large areas with sparse vegetation, plant density appeared to be a function of seasonal soil moisture and soil texture rather than the intensity of grazing.

Fifth, we also collected data from grazing exclosures, that is to say, we fenced off areas at the beginning of the growing season and compared the amount of vegetation at the end of the season inside the ungrazed area with that outside at the end of the growing season. In 12 of the exclosures the amount outside was almost the same as that inside, and in the four where the amount was only 50% of the ungrazed total, we discovered that livestock pass through this area on their way to their daily watering and thus it is bound to be heavily grazed and trampled even under the most careful grazing management. These data, therefore, also suggest that overgrazing is not present, although a longer time frame covering several years is necessary for exclosures to accurately analyze the situation.

Our evidence suggests strongly that the government's decision to force the Pala nomads to reduce their herd size was unwarranted. Not only has there been no increase in herd size since commune dissolution in 1981, we found no evidence of overgrazing and pasture degradation. This does not mean that further longitudinal measurements will not reveal problems in Pala or that they do not already exist in other areas, but it does mean that one cannot simply assume that the nomads' verbalized goal to increase the number of their animals necessarily results in such an increase and, in turn, environmental destruction. Indeed, as others have started to assert, it is time to reevaluate past judgments and give more credit to traditional pastoral systems.

The combination of prejudice against the nomads' traditional system of production and management (i.e., the view that it is destructive and not worthy of serious consideration), coupled with a genuine, well-intended belief in Western notions of "conservation," has inadvertently created in Tibet a situation that is detrimental and threatening to the way of life of the nomadic pastoralists. It has fostered the belief that there is no need to implement a serious program to measure "carrying capacity" and monitor range utilization and vegetation condition, and has induced the government to impose per-capita livestock limits and to develop plans to modernize what it considers the nomads' "irrational" production system. Our data demonstrate that the government's assumptions and census information are flawed in Pala, and suggest that they may be flawed in other areas as well. Consequently, we consider it essential that systematic research be conducted on the current ecological status of the western Changtang before additional drastic measures such as the introduction of new species of livestock and vegetation are imposed on the nomads in the name of science and progress. While protecting Tibet's unique Changtang is not only a Chinese but a world concern, protection of the indigenous nomadic pastoralists who reside there is an equally important concern. It would be indeed ironic if after surviving the destructive Cultural Revolution, these nomads' way of life was destroyed by modern notions of "conservation" and "development" that are based on faulty evidence and flawed assumptions.

AFTERWORD: THE STATUS OF NOMADIC PASTORALISM IN PALA, 1986–88

THE NEW CHINESE ECONOMIC AND CULTURAL POLICIES implemented in Tibet in the 1980s have produced a major transformation in Pala. Following commune dissolution, the nomads' economy immediately reverted to the traditional household system of production and management which, enhanced by the concession on taxes, has led to an overall improvement in the standard of living, despite the fact that local-level officials have not completely implemented an open-market system. The new policies have also led to increasing involvement in the market economy and dramatic social and economic differentiation.

Equally important, the policies of the 1980s have fostered a cultural and social revitalization that has allowed the nomads to rebuild the foundations of their traditional way of life and openly express their commitment to traditional values and customs. These reforms created the conditions whereby the nomadic pastoralists of Pala were able to regain control of their lives as individuals and recreate for themselves a matrix of values, norms, and beliefs that are psychologically and culturally meaningful.

Despite their lack of confidence in Beijing's long-term commitment to the new policies and their perception of vulnerability vis-a-vis the arbitrary and sometimes exploitive practices of the government's representatives, life in Pala today is closer to the traditional era than at any time since China assumed direct administrative control over Tibet in 1959 and began to implement changes. With no Han Chinese officials to deal with, and Tibetan written and spoken language their medium of interaction with the government, there is no day-to-day reminder of ethnic subordination and conflict.

The new policies have, in essence, vindicated the nomads' belief in the worth of their nomadic way of life and their Tibetan ethnicity. The nomads of Pala like their way of life and want to maintain it in the years ahead, choosing to incorporate or ignore new items as they see fit. They want nothing more than to be allowed to pursue the life of their ancestors, and flourish or fail as the gods and their own abilities dictate. Although there are problems and issues yet to be resolved, for now, and for the foreseeable future, the nomadic pastoral way of life is alive and well on the Changtang —and all of us are richer for it.

NOTES

1 The "a" in Changtang is pronounced equivalent to the English "a" in f<u>a</u>ther. Unless otherwise noted, all Tibetan letters "a" are pronounced this way.

2 Pastoralists are people who subsist by raising livestock. Ranchers, therefore, are pastoralists. Nomadic pastoralists are people who not only subsist by raising livestock, but move with their herds to different pastures during the year, normally living in tents.

3 The TAR is almost exactly the same geographic area as the realm ruled by the Dalai Lama in the 1930 and '40s.

4 The "o" in *drok* is pronounced like the "o" in so, and the "a" in "ba" like the "a" in alone.

5 Not all monasteries, however, had estates with subjects. In Pala, for example, a small monastery of about 30 monks known as Tongling subsisted by leasing out to nomads the 1,600 female sheep and goats it had obtained over the years as gifts. It used a common lease system called "No birth, No death." This meant that the person who took the 1,600 animals had a fixed amount of butter (about a kilogram per animal) and wool to pay annually regardless of births or deaths to these animals. If the herd increased, the lessee profited since he still had to only pay for the 1,600 original animals. But if the herd decreased, he lost since he was still responsible for the fee for the original 1,600 animals.

6 So scant is the early new growth that it is common to see sheep and goats busily digging the loose topsoil with their feet to get at the new vegetation growing just below the surface.

7 With the exception of a few head of breeding stock, all male *nor* are castrated. The term yak, therefore, actually refers to castrated males, *bo-a* being the term for uncastrated breeding males.

8 A. Wallace. "Revitalization Movements." *American Anthropologist*. Vol. 58, 1956.

GLOSSARY

ba	*tsamba* balls
bo-a	stud yak
chü	district
chigye	foreigner
döja	women's black make-up
Drabye	name of salt flat
dri	female yak
drokba	nomadic pastoralist
drong	wild yak
gersha	private animals during commune
gowa	Tibetan gazelle
gurum	hard molasses cake
gyenlo	name of Red Guard group
kabrang	satellite encampment
kulu	cashmere
lokbar	nomads' basic garment
mangtso	"the masses"
marke	pasture unit in old society
Motso Pünnyi	Two Sisters Lake
na	blue sheep
naki	blue sheep hunting dog
ngatsab	a social class—"representatives of the lord"
nor	generic name for yak
nyamdre	name of Red Guard group
poba	wooden drinking cup
pöda	farmer
rima	sheep and goat dung
rogre	"mutual-aid" groups
shang	village administrative unit
shen	county
shima	home-base encampment
sho	yogurt
tsamba	flour made by grinding popped barley grains
tü	mixture of butter, cheese, hard molasses and *tsamba*
yö	popped whole grain barley

INDEX

ACKNOWLEDGEMENTS

THIS STUDY WAS CONDUCTED in collaboration with the Tibet Academy of Social Sciences, whose scholars we wish to thank for their advice and superb assistance. We also want to thank the various local Tibetan officials for their cooperation, our field assistants for their extraordinary help and insight, and last but not least, the people of Pala who endured our endless questions and measurements with the good humor and dignity that typify their way of life. Funding was provided by The National Academy of Sciences' Committee for Scholarly Communication with the People's Republic of China (the National Program for Advanced Research and Study in China), the National Geographic Society's Committee for Research and Exploration, and the National Science Foundation. We also deeply appreciate the support of Wilbur E. Garrett, Editor of the *National Geographic Magazine* who first suggested that we try to put together an article on our research and provided film, processing and invaluable technical advice that led both to the June 1989 article in that magazine, and this book. Our thanks also go to William Graves and William Allen, our remarkable *National Geographic* text and illustrations editors, whose insightful suggestions and encouragement played a major role in bringing this project to fruition. Finally, we also thank our current editors Magnus Bartlett and Deke Castleman, and designer David Hurst for their work and encouragement in the construction of this book.

Melvyn C. Goldstein and Cynthia M. Beall
Case Western Reserve University
Cleveland, Ohio
September 28, 1989

Cynthia Beall

Mel Goldstein